FIRST CHRISTMAS

Books by Paul L. Maier

A MAN SPOKE, A WORLD LISTENED

PONTIUS PILATE

FIRST CHRISTMAS

FIRST CHRISTMAS

The True and Unfamiliar Story in Words and Pictures

Paul L. Maier

HARPER & ROW, PUBLISHERS

NEW YORK, EVANSTON, SAN FRANCISCO, LONDON

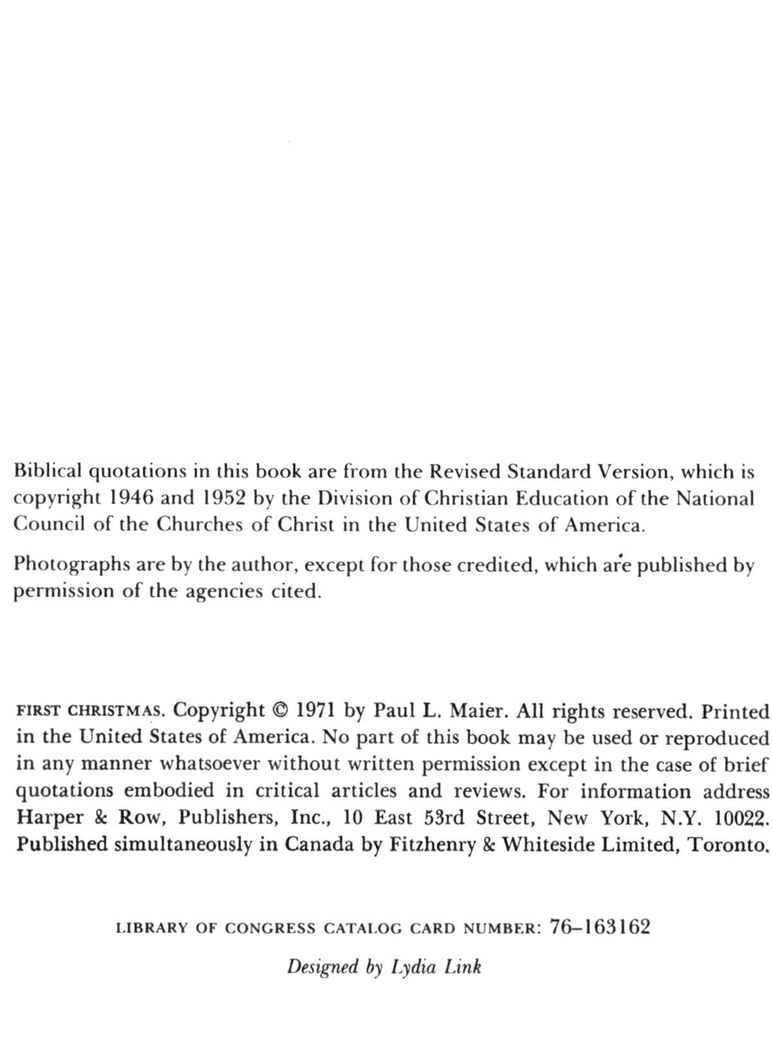

Biblical quotations in this book are from the Revised Standard Version, which is copyright 1946 and 1952 by the Division of Christian Education of the National Council of the Churches of Christ in the United States of America.

Photographs are by the author, except for those credited, which are published by permission of the agencies cited.

LIBRARY OF CONGRESS CATALOG CARD NUMBER: 76–163162

Designed by Lydia Link

FOR

Larry and Jan Harding

CONTENTS

ILLUSTRATIONS

COLOR PLATES

PREFACE

Although little is known of the birth of Jesus Christ outside the New Testament, the full story of the first Christmas is not limited to the Gospels of Matthew and Luke. Many important aspects of the event come into sharper focus when history, geography, archaeology, and even astronomy shed their light on the Nativity.

In offering this evidence, these chapters deal less with the familiar story of Jesus' birth and more with its background. They try to tell the *un*familiar story of the first Christmas by exploring the nooks and crannies of the past for fresh information and interesting sidelights on the Nativity. Stripping away the layers of legend and folklore which nineteen centuries have imposed on the famous event, this Christmas documentary will aim to tell "how it really was" in the world of the Nativity, providing some insights which are well known, some little known, and some new. No liberties were taken with the facts, which are documented in the Notes at the end of the book, most of which involve original sources.

I am especially indebted to Thorpe Menn, Book Editor of *The Kansas City Star,* for having suggested the theme of this book, which grew out of a seven-part Christmas feature series in the *Star,* as well as to Donald D. Jones, the City Editor, for having commissioned me to write the original articles, since expanded into book form.

P.L.M.

Western Michigan University

FIRST CHRISTMAS

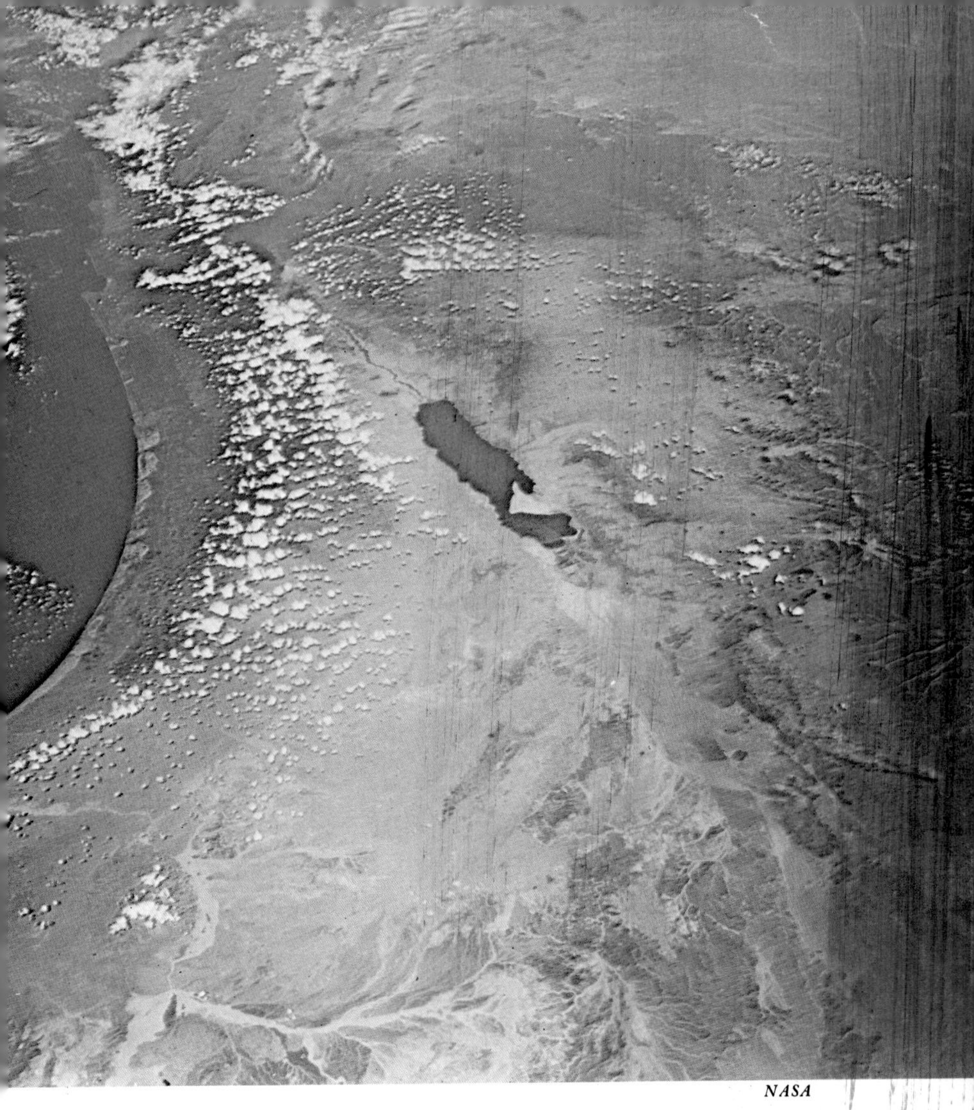

NASA

All of Palestine and most of the Negev are visible in this photograph taken by the Apollo 7 mission in October, 1968, with astronauts Schirra, Cunningham, and Eisele. The Sea of Galilee, half beclouded, the Jordan River, and the Dead Sea are in the left center of the picture. The Mediterranean lies at the extreme left, just above the Sinai desert.

D. Rubinger, Israel Ministry of Tourism

An aerial view of Bethlehem, looking eastward over the Church of the Nativity in the Center toward the hills of Judea. *(Opposite Upper:)* The interior nave of the Church of the Nativity. *(Opposite Lower:)* Christmas Eve illumination, looking from the Church of the Nativity out to Manger Square in Bethlehem.

Matson Photo Service

A. Lieberman, Israel Gov't. Tourist Office, Chicago

The city of Nazareth in Galilee, where Jesus spent his boyhood years. Peeking just over the ridge at the left center is the summit of Mt. Tabor, where the Transfiguration presumably took place. To the right is the Plain of Esdraelon.

The Politics of the First Christmas

1

A CAESAR'S CENSUS

In those days a decree went out from Caesar Augustus that all the world should be enrolled. . . . And all went to be enrolled, each to his own city. And Joseph also went up from Galilee, from the city of Nazareth, to Judea, to the city of David, which is called Bethlehem, because he was of the house and lineage of David, to be enrolled with Mary, his betrothed, who was with child.

LUKE 2:1–5

THE FIRST PERSON MENTIONED in Luke's familiar story of Christmas was neither Palestinian, nor Jew, nor shepherd, nor wise man. In fact, he would seem to have had nothing at all to do with the story, for he was the Roman emperor, Caesar Augustus. And yet it was his decision, 1,500 miles away in Rome, which started the train of events that finally led to the birth of Jesus in Bethlehem.

Under normal circumstances, Jesus would have been born in Nazareth, the home of Joseph and Mary. But, as Luke explains, Augustus decreed an enrollment or census of his vast empire, and all subjects of Rome had to return for registration at their ancestral home towns. Since both Joseph and Mary were distant descendants of the much-married King David, they prepared to travel down to David's city, the sleepy little town of Bethlehem in the sere and arid Judean hills six miles southwest of Jerusalem.

Was This Trip Necessary?

That Mary ever had to endure the rigors of this eighty-mile journey on the back of a jogging donkey while in a state of very advanced pregnancy has been doubted by some scholars. Rome never required her subjects to return to their original homes for such enrollments, they claim, and Luke must have garbled his facts. But this view has been disproved by the discovery of a Roman census edict from 104 A.D. in neighboring Egypt, in which taxpayers who were living elsewhere were ordered to return to their original homes for registration.

An obscure Galilean couple had to obey a distant Caesar because sixty years earlier, the Roman general Pompey had conquered Palestine, and the land orbited perforce into the Roman universe. Currently, it was under Rome's control as a "client kingdom" ruled by a local king, Herod the Great, who was directly responsible to the Roman emperor.

Augustus himself, the grandnephew and adopted heir of Julius Caesar, was Rome's first emperor. His fascinating career began in the bloody civil wars of the late Roman republic, continued beyond a victorious showdown with his arch rival Mark Antony, and culminated in a lengthy era of peace and prosperity, well styled the *Pax Augusta,* for Augustus created and preserved the happy concord throughout the forty-four years of his rule.

Less familiar than the vaunted glories of Augustus' reign—the conquered lands and kings, or the Rome he transformed from brick into marble—is the man's intriguing religious policy. Had he not been emperor, Caesar Augustus might well have gone down in history as a religious reformer, for he tried to revive the drooping interest in Rome's state religion. By his day, the average Roman had abandoned his beliefs in the gods of Greco-Roman mythology and philosophical skepticism was growing, while the more credulous joined the foreign mystery cults that had invaded the Empire. Augustus, however, felt that this neglect

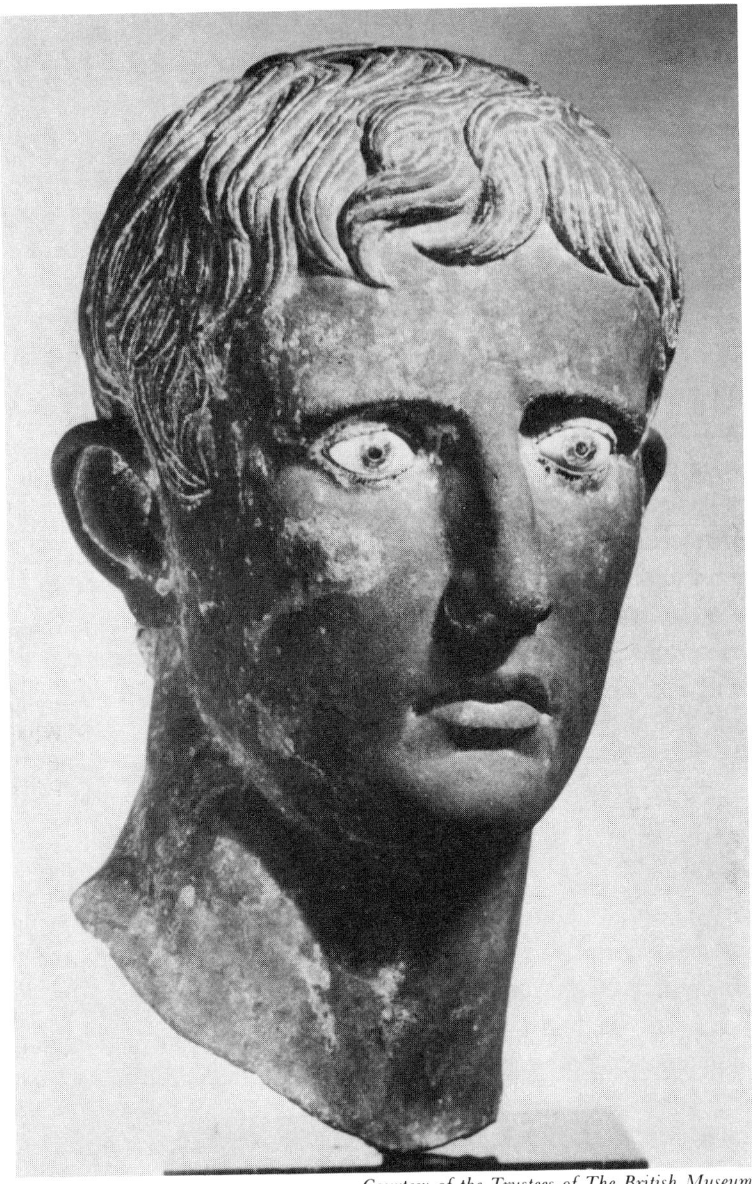

Courtesy of the Trustees of The British Museum

This bronze head of Augustus, portraying him at the age of thirty, was discovered near the Nile River at Merowe in the Sudan.

of the gods was demoralizing Roman society, and that only a restoration of the old republican piety would preserve her greatness.

So he set about his religious revival with enthusiasm. He fairly rained temples and shrines down on the Empire, restoring eighty-two temples in the city of Rome alone. He became *pontifex maximus* ("highest priest") in the state cult, and tried to spark a moral renewal in society.

Too Many Bachelors

Many Roman men and women of the time were indulging in a very easy morality to escape what they called "the tedium of marriage," and soon marital and birth rates had dwindled alarmingly. One day, Augustus was disturbed enough to stalk into the Forum and devise a crude test of the situation: he told a crowd of men gathered there to separate into two groups, the bachelors on one side, the married men on the other. The handful of husbands was so much smaller that he launched into an anguished harangue against the bachelors, which began, classically:

> What shall I call you? *Men?* But you aren't fulfilling the duties of men. *Citizens?* But for all your efforts, the city is perishing. *Romans?* But you are in the process of blotting out this name altogether! . . . What humanity would be left if all the rest of mankind should do what you are doing? . . . *You are committing murder* in not fathering in the first place those who ought to be your descendants!

. . . and on to other such gems of imperial logic.

Augustus followed this bluster with legislation designed to reverse the tide by making promiscuity a crime, while conferring political advantages on a father of three children. Bachelors who shirked "the duty of marriage" were penalized in their right to inherit, and they could not even secure good seats at the games! The bachelors, of course, tried to circumvent such penalties by "marrying" infant girls, but Augustus quickly countered by setting the minimum age for engagement at ten for girls, with a two-year upper limit for length of courtship.

Perhaps it was to gauge his success in raising the marriage and birth rates that Augustus was so concerned about the imperial census, and he took several, as in the Christmas story, during his lengthy reign. Such enrollments, of course, were also the basis for the Roman system of taxation. Later census returns showed a considerable increase in population, though this may have been due as much to the return of peace and prosperity after all the bloodshed of Rome's civil wars as to Augustus' legislation. But the emperor was pleased enough with the results that he proudly mentioned his censuses in eighth place among the thirty-five "Acts of Augustus" for which he wished to be remembered, items that were later engraved on two bronze plaques outside his mausoleum.

Unfortunately, he reported figures only for that privileged group in the Empire known as male Roman citizens:

The census	of	28 B.C.	showed	4,063,000	Roman	citizens
"	"	8 B.C.	"	4,233,000	"	"
"	"	14 A.D.	"	4,937,000	"	"

At this time, however, the entire Roman Empire—like Luke, the Romans also hyperbolized it as "the whole world"—would have numbered almost 55,000,000 people.

The census mentioned in the Christmas story was probably a provincial enrollment associated with the citizens' census of 8 B.C., but apparently the machinery necessary to take it in far-off Palestine was not prepared until about 5 B.C., since 8 B.C. is some three years too early for the birth of Christ. (For reasons that will be explained in a later chapter, Jesus was *not* born in 1 A.D.)

An Unknown Subject

One might wonder how Augustus would have reacted to this Judean census in which—had he chosen to examine the returns from Bethlehem—the following group of three names would have been included:

When Jesus was born, the entire Mediterranean world was governed from Rome. The ruins of her ancient Forum still stand, and this view looks over the Pool of the Vestal Virgins to the place where Julius Caesar's body was cremated (right center) and the rectangular reconstructed Senate house beyond.

Joseph Ben-Iacob, carpenter
Mary Bath-Ioachim, his wife
Yeshua or Jesus, first-born son

Did Augustus ever even see the names? The chances are virtually nil. Certainly he never learned the significance of what had happened in Bethlehem because of his decision to take the census.

At the time of Augustus' death in 14 A.D., Jesus was about nineteen years old, an apprentice carpenter in Nazareth, and the emperor still could not possibly have heard of him. He would have been astounded to know that later ages would assign his own death to the year 14 A.D. ("in the year of the Lord") rather than the Roman date, 767 A.U.C. (*ab urbe condita,* "from the founding of the city") all because of that unknown subject, born in Bethlehem. And he would have been amazed that future generations would wish each other a "Merry Christmas" rather than *"Io Saturnalia!"*—that great end-of-the-year festival in Rome which featured pagan delights and many of the holiday trappings of our secular yuletide, including holly, mistletoe, and evergreens, the exchange of gifts, and much feasting and drinking.

But the successors of the emperor and of the baby would discover each other soon enough.

The Land of the First Christmas

2

PALESTINE THE PARADOX

Now the Lord said to Abram, "Go from your country . . . to the land that I will show you. And I will make of you a great nation. . . . To your descendants I will give this land."

GENESIS 12:1, 2, 7

PALESTINE IS A LAND rippling with irony. It gave birth to two great religions and nurtured a third, yet it may be the most bitterly contested spot on earth. Jews, Christians, and Muslims all call it the Holy Land, but probably more blood has been spilled there per acre than anywhere else in the world. The ancient Hebrews claimed it as their Promised Land because of the divine pledge to Abraham, and yet they had to fight the Philistines to win it. And then they saw it crushed by invading Assyrians and Babylonians, mauled by Egyptians, torn by Syrians, and finally conquered by Romans.

But this is merely the record up to the time of the first Christmas, when the baby called "The Prince of Peace" was born. After that, the land was assaulted by the Persians, Arabs, Crusaders, Mamelukes, Turks, and British, while today it smolders with Arab-Israeli hostilities.

Why this sickening saga of bloodshed? One prime reason is because the three major faiths of Western civilization regard Palestine as their own religious cradle, and each, at one time or another, has taken up arms against the other two "strangers in the nursery." To Jews it is the land of the sacred Torah; to Christians, that of the Old and New Testaments; and to Muslims

Israel Gov't. Tourist Office

The Dead Sea, looking eastward over the fortress-rock of Masada. Originally a stronghold of Herod the Great, Masada was the citadel where Jewish rebels put themselves to death rather than submit to the might of Rome in 73 A.D.

it is Abraham's country—they also claim him as patriarch through his son Ishmael—while Jerusalem marks the spot, so they teach, where Mohammed's steed last touched earth before ascending into heaven with the prophet on his back.

But blame for the bloodshed must also be deposited squarely at the doors of geography and politics. Palestine has the glory of being located at the juncture of two continents—Africa and Asia—and so served as the crossroads of antiquity. But this strategic location also proved a heavy burden. The armies of the ancient world, even if they had no quarrel with the people of Palestine, regularly used the land as a causeway en route to attacking each other, ravaging Palestine in the process. The inhabitants had as much safety as would a flock of sparrows that chose to build their nests on a superhighway.

Overrun, despoiled, devastated, and small—roughly the size and shape of a Vermont twisted upside down—Palestine still exerted probably the most powerful influence on subsequent civilization, per capita, of any land in history. Her Hebrew inhabitants gave the world monotheism and a system of ethics that has not been superseded—which law on any of the nations' lawbooks is not a corollary of one of the Ten Commandments?—and her Christians seeded a faith that is believed by nearly a billion people today. As has well been said, Western civilization is like a family whose mother was Hebrew, whose father was Greek, and that moved away to live in Rome.

A Geographic Marvel

Even if it had no religious significance, Palestine would be an intriguing land. In fact, it is an earth scientist's paradise, boasting a Sea of Galilee which is almost 700 feet *below* sea level and a wriggling stream called the Jordan that channels Galilee's fresh water and empties it into an oblong, finger-shaped basin of brackish fluid known as the Dead Sea. Jordan means "descender," an appropriate name for its own 600-foot drop, and yet it is hardly a straight gorge, for it twists and loops some 200 miles to make the 65-mile trip from Galilee to the Dead Sea as the crow flies.

The Dead Sea is 1,286 feet below sea level, and if some mad engineer cut a canal up to the Mediterranean, the whole Jordan valley would soon be overwhelmed with a quivering mass of water a quarter-mile high. The Dead Sea basin is quite literally the lowest place in the world, six times as far below sea level as Death Valley in California. (The lowest spot on the earth's crust is the sea bottom within the Marianas trench in the Pacific Ocean, where soundings have reached an ocean depth of more than 36,000 feet.) At least 25 per cent salt and other minerals—compared with 5 per cent for the ocean—the Dead Sea is so dense that a swimmer can barely submerge in it and is flipped to the surface like a cork. Fish leaving the Jordan delta waters die within minutes after swimming into the Dead Sea, and the evaporation rate is so fierce that it equals the incoming flow of the Jordan.

Even the underground regions here rumble with a separate fascination of their own. Underlying the whole depression are subterranean gases and volcanic activity which bubble up hot springs and asphalt, and periodically cause earthquakes. These phenomena may well have been responsible for the fall of those famed sin capitals in Old Testament times, Sodom and Gomorrah.

More than anything else, Palestine resembles an accordion-fold of land, with four diverse bands running north and south. Bordering the Mediterranean to the west is a flat and fertile coastal plain; next to it rises a central hilly plateau on which Jerusalem and Bethlehem are located; beyond that plunges the Great Rift valley of the Jordan and the Dead Sea; and finally, the tablelands of the Transjordan rise abruptly to the east.

But political lines directly crisscrossed this geography at the time of the birth of Christ, dividing the land into three bands running east and west: rolling, verdant Galilee to the north, the picturesque home of Joseph and Mary; Samaria in the center, the bleached land of those despised half-breed cousins of the Jews called the Samaritans; and Judea to the south, the more barren and hilly religious and political center of the land. Because of their trip down to Bethlehem, the subsequent flight to Egypt, and their eventual return to Nazareth, the Holy Family would traverse the greater part of Palestine before the Christmas story reached its conclusion.

A White Christmas?

What kind of weather they would have encountered has evoked the widest range of guesses. Old sixteenth-century European woodcuts show Joseph and Mary all bundled up, braving the blizzards of a north German winter on the way to Bethlehem. But even aside from the humorous thought of a snowstorm in a subtropical climate, it is by no means certain that the Nativity even took place in the winter months.

But, assuming for the moment that it did, *could* the first have been a white Christmas? This is highly improbable, certainly, but by no means as impossible as many insist. Snow does fall in the Jerusalem area about three or four days each winter, and some-

The River Jordan, near the place where Jesus was baptized.

times in considerable quantity: in January, 1950, twenty inches fell; in February, 1920, twenty-nine inches. The meteorology, then, would allow a very remote possibility of snow at Bethlehem on that day which would shift history.

Palestine lies between 31° and 33° north latitude, in the same parallel as Georgia, Arizona, Nagasaki, and Shanghai. But since it is adjacent to that great climatic storage battery called the Mediterranean Sea, its weather is moderate and two-seasonal: a cool but not uncomfortable winter, when some rain falls; and a summer in which sun often shines 98 per cent of the daytime.

However, because of the wide variety in the forms and altitude of its tortured terrain, ranging from 9,230-foot Mt. Hermon in the north to the subthalassic Dead Sea depression, from fertile vales to blazing deserts, local climates in Palestine can vary from subarctic to torrid. Some have even suggested that one reason the Bible is intelligible nearly everywhere in the world is because Palestine offers a bit of almost all the geographic and climatic conditions on earth. At least there is reason enough for the pictorial variety offered on Christmas cards displaying backgrounds from the Holy Land that seem to clash.

3

A GALILEAN COUPLE

Now the birth of Jesus Christ took place in this way. When his mother Mary had been betrothed to Joseph, before they came together she was found to be with child by the Holy Spirit.

MATTHEW 1:18

NAZARETH IS USUALLY the forgotten town in the Christmas story, but this is where it all began. The Galilean village was indeed a very forgettable place in ancient times. Astonishingly, there is no mention of Nazareth in the Old Testament or the Talmud, and later on one of Jesus' future disciples would sneer, "Can anything good come out of Nazareth?" (Jn. 1:46).

"Indeed!" the world has since replied, not only because of the impressive figure of Jesus but also the very beautiful story of his origin. Nestled in one of the hills of lower Galilee overlooking the triangular Plain of Esdraelon, Nazareth was an insignificant village far smaller than the present bustling city of 20,000. Its secluded inhabitants had to travel northward over four miles of back roads to get to Sepphoris in order to purchase the many items not available in Nazareth.

This is where Joseph would get whatever carpenter's tools and supplies he had not inherited from his father. The Gospels tell us very little about Joseph, but if he resembled the pious, hardworking class of his Jewish colleagues in Galilee, he would not think of marriage until he was at least twenty-five years old. On the other hand, it was customary for girls to marry shortly after puberty, and how this young craftsman became engaged to a

fourteen- or fifteen-year-old girl named Mary is not recorded. Certainly they must some time have met at one of the harvest festivals if not at the village well in Nazareth—it was the sole source of water supply—and in a hamlet the size of Nazareth, everyone knew everyone else.

Romance and courtship did not play a large role in ancient times, and most marriages were arranged between the parents of the couple. On the other hand, bride and groom were not simply thrown at each other in a loveless match. Directly or indirectly, their comments and conduct often alerted parents as to which family to contact, and love was indeed a factor in many of the alliances.

The Engagement

What most probably happened was this. One day, Joseph asked his parents if he could marry that village girl who was his distant relative, Mary. They discussed it among themselves before giving him an answer, carefully appraising Mary's parentage, ancestry, and resources. The last, of course, was not a prime consideration, since everyone in Nazareth was poor. And they could hardly fault Mary's background, for it was the same as their own: although humble, both families were distant descendants of the royal family of Israel, and they could proudly trace their family tree back to King David and one of his many wives. They easily approved Joseph's choice, probably with enthusiasm.

Then Joseph's father paid a call on Mary's parents, who would act duly surprised as the purpose of the visit grew plain. But Mary's random comments about the young carpenter Joseph had all but shouted her interest, and so the discussion began in earnest, the two fathers doing most of the negotiating. In Biblical times, marriage was considered a covenant between two families, not just the bridal pair, so there were many matters to discuss besides dowry, which would have been small in any case.

Finally the fathers happily agreed to a marriage contract be-

Israel Information Service

The Church of the Annunciation in Nazareth, built over the presumed site where Mary was confronted by the angel.

tween their children. Joseph was then brought before Mary, and their parents uttered a formal benediction over them as they tasted a cup of wine together. This, the legal betrothal, was far more binding than the modern engagement. Only divorce could break it, and even though they were not yet married, had either Joseph or Mary been unfaithful to each other, it would have been deemed an adultery punishable by death. Had Joseph died in the meantime, Mary would have been his legal widow.

Since betrothal was nearly tantamount to marriage, could the couple enjoy lawful sexual relations? There is some evidence that engaged Judean couples could and did exercise this privilege, even though both still lived at home with their parents. In the more conservative Galilean countryside, however, virginity was maintained until the wedding itself, which laid great stress on prior purity. In the case of Joseph and Mary, the New Testament is explicit in stating that Joseph did not know Mary sexually until after the birth of Jesus (Mt. 1:24 f.).

The Annunciation

One day, during the months between her engagement and marriage, Mary's wedding preparations were momentously interrupted. Luke tells the familiar story of the angel Gabriel appearing to Mary with the words: "Hail, O favored one, the Lord is with you! . . . And behold, you will conceive in your womb and bear a son, and you shall call his name Jesus. He will be great, and will be called the Son of the Most High . . . and of his kingdom there will be no end."

One reason many moderns doubt the story, quite apart from the angel, is because any such apparition should have frightened the poor girl out of her wits. And yet Mary was brought up immediately after Old Testament times, in which angelic visits were commonplace, her elders reported. So her immediate reaction was quite logical indeed: "How can this be, since I have no husband?"

"The Holy Spirit will come upon you," Luke records the angel's reply, "and the power of the Most High will overshadow you; therefore the child to be born will be called holy, the Son of God."

Mary agreed in simple trust. "Behold, I am the handmaid of the Lord: let it be to me according to your word" (Lk. 1:26 ff.).

Under the assumption that it must have taken even a divine-human baby the normal term to develop, Christendom appointed March 25 (exactly nine months before December 25) as the Feast of the Annunciation, when Jesus was also conceived. The emphasis, however, is not on any calendar precision—the exact date of the Nativity is unknown—but on the commemoration itself.

For Mary, the news that she would bear the long-awaited Messiah who had been promised her people was both joyful and staggering. It filled her with a sense of wonder to which she finally gave expression in the *Magnificat,* spoken at the home of her cousin Elizabeth, mother of John the Baptist, whom she visited shortly after the Annunciation. Her exultant words began, "My soul magnifies the Lord, and my spirit rejoices in God my Savior. . . ." and they would become part of the Christian liturgy (Lk. 1:46 ff.).

But Mary's pregnancy was cruel and shocking news to Joseph, for he knew that he was not the father. Probably he could not really believe Mary's story of the angelic visit, so he had to agonize a decision between three options: (1) marry the girl quickly, and hope the tongues in Nazareth would someday stop wagging over a six-month baby; (2) publicly divorce Mary as an adulteress, in which case she would have been stoned to death; or (3) have the marriage contract set aside quietly, while Mary went off to have her baby elsewhere.

Being a good and pious sort, Joseph would not marry an adulteress, but he loved Mary too much to wish her public shame and death. So he quickly decided on the third alternative. But then, as Matthew recorded it, there was another angelic interposition in the Christmas story:

> . . . An angel of the Lord appeared to him in a dream, saying, "Joseph, son of David, do not fear to take Mary your wife, for that which is conceived in her is of the Holy Spirit; she will bear a son, and you shall call his name Jesus, for he will save his people from their sins." (Mt. 1:20)

How easily Mary's story jibed after such an experience! Now sharing his betrothed's incredible secret, Joseph could bury his suspicions and anxieties and marry his beloved as soon as possible.

The Marriage

Probably no more than a week or two afterward, the wedding was celebrated in Nazareth. From various clues scattered across the Bible, it seems that Palestinian nuptials were more similar to modern weddings than different from them. The two bridal parties marched in procession, accompanied by music, to the place where they would be married, the bride and groom wearing garlands and jewelry, and the bride a veil too. There were attendants on both sides, and a wedding feast followed which could be quite elaborate. Samson's nuptial banquet lasted for seven days (Judg. 14:12), but such affairs in Nazareth were always on a smaller scale.

For the next five months, Mary lived happily at Joseph's house, her pregnancy now obvious. One day came the news about the Roman emperor's edict requiring all his subjects to enroll themselves for the census at their ancestral homes. However much they must have dreaded the prospect of a four- or five-day trip down to Bethlehem when she was in advanced pregnancy, Joseph and Mary quickly realized that Augustus' decree very nicely solved two formidable problems for them. They could never go to Bethlehem and return again before Jesus' birth, so he would now have to be born in Judea, and any prying neighbors in Nazareth need never know that theirs was apparently a six-month baby. At this stage, it would have been useless to try to explain to them the wonderful kind of child this really was.

The other difficulty concerned the familiar prophecy that the Messiah was to be born in Bethlehem. In fact, it was the only cloud smudging Mary's happiness, for if she were indeed to bear the Christ, why had God chosen a girl living in Nazareth rather than Bethlehem? The news from Rome easily placed the last piece of the divine-human puzzle into place. Even though Joseph alone could have attended to the census obligations in Bethlehem, Mary had every reason to make the trip also.

Commending their few valuables to his father's keeping, Joseph and Mary gathered their necessities and set out for Bethlehem. The picture of Joseph tenderly guiding the donkey on which Mary was sitting—a little apprehensive lest the birth pangs come too early—is so enshrined in imagination, art, and literature that it needs no further comment.

What route they chose for the trip south is not so graphic and definite. It could well have been the central route via the valleys winding through the hills of Samaria, which was the shortest. On the other hand, if the pious Joseph wanted to avoid any contact with the Samaritans or wished to keep Mary warm during a chill time of the year, he could have chosen an alternate route southeast across the Plain of Esdraelon, down the Jordan River valley as far as Jericho, and then up to Jerusalem and Bethlehem.

In either case, Mary would suffer discomforts on this eighty- or ninety-mile journey—the legends that she was miraculously spared them are all apocryphal—but she would soon forget the pain in joy at the extraordinary thing about to happen to her. The birth of any child is a marvel of its own, but that of a divine child, as she firmly believed hers to be, was an incalculable wonder.

The Time of the First Christmas

4

AN UNDATABLE DATE

But when the time had fully come, God sent forth his Son, born of woman, born under the law, to redeem those who were under the law, so that we might receive adoption as sons.

GALATIANS 4:4–5

PAUL'S FAMOUS COMMENT that the Nativity happened "in the fullness of time," as the original Greek has it, is usually interpreted to mean that God had a good sense of timing, since conditions prevailing in the Mediterranean world could not have been more ripe for the spread of Christianity. The Old Testament had predicted the birth of a Messiah for centuries, and the Greeks had given their world a universal language through which Jesus' message could spread easily and quickly. The Roman Empire had organized the whole Mediterranean basin into one vast communications network, almost perfectly geared to foster the spread of Christianity, since its missionaries could travel from city to city without fear of piracy at sea or brigands by land. Rome had also spread the welcome blanket of peace across the world, the *Pax Romana,* a time in which the new faith could thrive.

And so the first Christmas happened "in the fullness of time" indeed. But precisely *when* was that time? Unfortunately, there is no exact answer. Ironically, the event that has divided our reckoning of time into years B.C. and A.D. is itself almost undatable. "Everyone knows" Jesus must have been born on December 25, A.D. 1, but it is not quite that simple, and certainly this date is wrong. For Herod the Great died in the spring of 4 B.C., and the

Israel Gov't. Tourist Office

The city of Jerusalem, looking eastward over the Dome of the Rock toward the Mount of Olives. The Dome marks the presumed spot where Abraham bound Isaac for sacrifice, where the Temple of Solomon was built, and where Mohammed supposedly ascended into heaven.

king was very much alive during the visit of the Magi in the Christmas story.* Therefore Jesus would have to have been born before this time, and his birth is usually set during the winter of 5–4 B.C. ("*B*efore *C*hrist," or, incredibly, "Before Himself").

Why, then, is our calendar four or five years off? Why is the present decade not 1970–80 but, literally, 1975–85 A.D. (*anno Domini,* "in the year of the Lord")?

It was a sixth-century Roman monk-mathematician-astronomer named Dionysius Exiguus (Dionysius the Little) who unknowingly committed what became history's greatest numerical error in terms of cumulative effect. For in reforming the calendar to pivot about the birth of Christ, he dated the Nativity in the year 753 from the founding of Rome, when in fact Herod died only 749 years after Rome's founding. The result of Dionysius' chronology, which remains current, was to give the correct traditional date for the founding of Rome, but one that is at least four or five years off for the birth of Christ.

While Jesus may have been born as early as 7 B.C., such earlier datings for the Nativity would make him a little too old for the "about thirty years of age" when he began his public ministry in 28–29 A.D. (Lk. 3:23). Unfortunately, it is not possible to work back to any exact date for Jesus' birth from any later information about his adult life.

The Season?

But surely the Christmas story provides other chronological clues. Luke tried to date the event with some precision in his famous prologue about Augustus' decree "that all the world should be enrolled. This was the first enrollment, when Quirinius

*Recently, the English scholar W. E. Filmer has suggested that Herod may have died as late as 1 B.C., but this alternate chronology has not been generally accepted, since it is too difficult to reconcile with the regnal dates of Herod's sons and successors. It seems that Herod did indeed die in 4 B.C.—For further detail on the chronology of Christmas, see the admirable study by Professor Jack Finegan, *Handbook of Biblical Chronology* (Princeton, 1964), pp. 215 ff.

was governor of Syria" (2:1–2). The solution, then, is merely to find the date for Augustus' imperial census, as well as the ruling dates for the Syrian governor Quirinius.

And how scholars have tried to do just that—and with what little success! The imperial citizens' census of 8 B.C., discussed in the first chapter, probably reached Palestine as a broadened provincial census anytime between that year and perhaps 6 or 5 B.C., as indicated, a range too broad for much help in pinpointing the time of the first Christmas.

But the governor of Syria, Publius Sulpicius Quirinius, is known from Roman records. He had been a consul, with military and business successes to his credit, though a chronic avarice stained his memory. But when was he governor of Syria? Not until 6–7 A.D., according to ancient records, which is ten years too late for the Nativity census, and Luke has been faulted for inaccuracy here. However, an archaeological inscription suggests that Quirinius may have had an earlier term as governor, or at least a special commission to carry out such a census, since he was in the East at the time, also as military commander. Other scholars suggest an alternate interpretation of Luke's text: "This census was first really carried out when Quirinius was governor of Syria," i.e., a decade later than the preliminary census during the reign of Herod.

What about the great Star of Bethlehem which attracted the wise men? Astral events are indeed prime props in any chronology, but astronomers have never agreed on exactly what the star may have been, so it is difficult to date it. (Nevertheless, the Star of Bethlehem is so fascinating a phenomenon in its own right that it will be discussed in a later chapter.) Adding up all the clues, hints, and shreds of evidence from every available source, many scholars set the date for the Nativity some time between the fall of 5 B.C. and March of 4 B.C.

Others maintain it must have happened in spring, because the shepherds were out in the fields, "keeping watch over their flock by night" at the angelic announcement (Lk. 2:8), which would suggest lambing time. Only then, presumably, did shepherds bother to guard their flocks at night. In the winter, sheep would have been in the corral.

This clue seems impressive enough, but it is by no means conclusive. In many of the rural districts of Palestine, the flocks were not fed in pens but had to forage for their food both in summer and winter. During the great winter snowfall of 1910–11 in Syria, hundreds of thousands of sheep died because snow covered the ground for weeks, interrupting their feeding. And a passage in the Jewish *Mishnah* states that some sheep pastured near Bethlehem were destined for sacrifice at the Temple in Jerusalem, and suggests that these flocks lay out in the fields all year around.

Since shepherding seems to be one of the least changed occupations in Palestine over the last two thousand years, it may be instructive to gauge the present practice. The famed Chautauqua and Lyceum lecturer, Stephen A. Haboush, the former "Shepherd Boy of Galilee," writes:

> As a boy, I kept our flock through the fall of the year and up to the first of January out among the low hills and valleys around the Sea of Galilee. But during the rainy season in January and February, I would keep the sheep in the fold back of our home in Tiberias. In Judea, however, where there is only half as much annual rainfall, the shepherds keep their flocks grazing out in the valleys for most of the months of the winter season, as I know from members of my tribe.

And Christmastime visitors to Bethlehem today tell of seeing shepherds out in the fields with their sheep, their heads muffled against the chilly weather in colorful *keffiyehs.*

The Day?

Why is Christmas celebrated on December 25? The early Christian church seems to have observed the birth of Christ on January 6 in the East, and on December 25 in the West, but both practices began too late—the 300's A.D.—to warrant attaching any precision to these dates.

Probably it was a matter of substitution. The Romans of the time not only celebrated their Saturnalia festival at the close of December, but they also thought that December 25 marked the date of the winter solstice (instead of December 21) when they observed the pagan feast of *Sol Invictus,* the Unconquerable Sun, which was just in the act of turning about to aim northward once again. Christianity sought to replace these pagan festivals with a Christian celebration honoring the "sun of righteousness," a common epithet for Jesus as Messiah. Yet Christmas, even with its Christian name, has never been able to shake off the secular part of this end-of-the-year festival. But all this should not obscure the fact that, according to the best reckoning, Jesus may indeed have been born in the winter of 5–4 B.C.

One could wish that an event of this importance were more precisely datable. Yet the ancients, especially in the Near East, had a less exacting view of time than did later ages with their accurate clocks and calendars. At a period when there was no universal system of chronology and events were dated "in the reign of King Such and Such" or "in the governorship of So and So," when numbers were often rounded off, and even the methods of counting years differed, perhaps it is fortunate to come within months of the actual date of the first Christmas. But the final paradox, certainly, is that something as imprecisely datable as the birth of Christ later served as the technical anchor date for the calendar used almost everywhere in the world today, which we find quite precise indeed.

Time, however, had a wholly different meaning for the pair just finishing that uncomfortable journey down to Bethlehem. The question nagging at Joseph and Mary as they threaded their way through that florid symphony of noise and color which was Jerusalem was this: would they reach Bethlehem in time for the event that now seemed imminent?

Trans World Airlines

Olive groves surround Bethlehem on the ridge beyond.

The Place of the First Christmas

5

A BETHLEHEM GROTTO

And while they were there, the time came for her to be delivered. And she gave birth to her first-born son and wrapped him in swaddling cloths, and laid him in a manger, because there was no place for them in the inn.

LUKE 2:6–7

IT IS ALMOST CERTAIN that Joseph and Mary reached Bethlehem in the late afternoon or early evening. Had they arrived earlier, lodging would not have been so difficult to find, although Bethlehem would have been crowded enough with the many descendants of King David returning to register at their ancestral home.

The picture of Joseph going from door to door, desperately begging shelter because Mary was in labor, has always struck a poignant chord amid the joy wreathing the rest of the Christmas story. And the nameless innkeeper who refused them refuge is usually enshrined next to Judas in the popular mind. But probably he—or was it his sympathetic wife?—remembered the cave behind the inn where animals were sheltered, and he threw it open to the hapless couple. The hills around Bethlehem are perforated with such caverns, and they are still used to shelter cattle and sheep. Grateful for any refuge in the crisis of his wife's birth pangs, Joseph carefully led the donkey and its precious burden down a steep path on the eastern side of the caravansary to the cave below it.

From all accounts of the Nativity, it seems that no one assisted Mary at the birth of Jesus—not even Joseph, for husbands were

KLM Royal Dutch Airlines

The modern city of Bethlehem, from the tower of the Church of the Nativity.

not to play the role of midwives. Self-delivery was by no means uncommon at the time. The women of Palestine, unlike neighboring mothers, prided themselves on delivering their babies rather easily and were quite able to take care of themselves in the absence of a midwife, though physicians and midwives were also regularly used. Luke simply relates that Mary gave birth to her first-born son, wrapped him in long swaddling bands, and laid him in a feeding trough, which must have had the sweetish, grainy smell of hay, barley, and oats.

And so the incredible paradox happened at Bethlehem: history's greatest figure was born, not in a palace or mansion, but in a cavern-stable. For Joseph and Mary, the holiest moment of all must have come before the shepherds paid their famous visit as they gazed at the extraordinary baby whose mission even they could scarcely comprehend. Small wonder that this has been the most familiar scene in all the florid history of art. Each generation, each school has attempted to portray the Nativity, with backgrounds ranging from Oriental to Italian to Flemish, and yet the tableau of the Holy Family in the Bethlehem grotto has remained an unconquered artistic challenge.

There is evidence that someone in Bethlehem relented and offered more normal accommodations to Joseph, Mary, and the newborn Jesus. For by the time the wise men arrived to present their gifts, the Holy Family seems to have been living in a "house" (Mt. 2:11). Or, as happens on any vacation trip today, the motel vacancies which are nonexistent the night a traveler arrives because he failed to call ahead for reservations quickly materialize the next day.

All Bethlehem must have rustled with news about "that poor girl from Galilee" who had no sooner arrived in town than she bore a child, since the shepherds and, later, the Magi had no trouble finding the Holy Family. Clearly, they must have been directed by the townspeople.

Jesus' birth in this particular town had vast implications for the people of Palestine. Bethlehem, which means "House of Bread,"

The doorway of the Church of the Nativity in Bethlehem is partially walled-up, permitting only children to enter without stooping. The Crusaders reduced the size of the entrance to prevent Arab horsemen from galloping into the interior.

Swissair

Israel Gov't. Tourist Office

The Church of the Nativity in Bethlehem, with entrance at the left center.

Swissair

The Grotto of the Nativity in Bethlehem, marking the traditional site where Christ was born.

A silver star on the marble floor of the Grotto of the Nativity presumably identifies the place where Jesus was born.

Israel Gov't. Tourist Office

was not only the setting for the story of Ruth, but it became the birthplace of David, and here the prophet Samuel anointed him King of Israel. Later it became the expected birthplace of that great "Son of David" or "Messiah" who was supposed to liberate the land from foreign control. It was no accident that over in Jerusalem, King Herod's priests came up with Bethlehem as the logical place to send the wise men for any newborn Christ, the Greek translation for the Hebrew Messiah.

The Site Today

"O little town of Bethlehem, how still we see thee lie. . . ." The lyrics fit not only the village of the first Christmas, but also the town of today. For two millennia seem to have brushed few changes into the Bethlehem scene. It remains a comparatively small town, six miles southwest of Jerusalem, and quiet enough —although the 20,000 who live there now have considerably increased its population from Jesus' day.

Today, the tourist almost always approaches Bethlehem from the north—the same direction as Joseph and Mary—on a curvy road that twists along a bleak ridge. From a final bend, just east of the city, the so-called Shepherds' Fields are pointed out, the presumed place where the herdsmen were watching their flocks at the time of the angelic announcement. The rolling slopes are covered with tawny grasses and dotted with drab scrubby bushes and some pines. Individual fields are fenced off by low stone walls or rows of silver-green olive trees.

The city itself is a maze of twisting cobblestone lanes, all of which seem to lead into the past. But they find a hub in the centrally located Manger Square, where the crowning sanctuary is the ancient Church of the Nativity, erected by the Byzantine emperor Justinian. This basilica is a less than impressive structure of whitish stone which seems to contrast too fiercely with the deep and often cloudless blue sky hanging over the town. A low, partially walled-up doorway compels a visitor to bend down upon entering the sanctuary.

Inside, the interior of the church is cool, dark, and hardly imposing, but parts of the nave date back to the time of Constantine, making this Christendom's oldest church in continuous use. Forty-four rose-colored columns with Corinthian capitals divide the nave from its two side aisles, and a round, shiny Christmas tree ornament dangles from each of its lighting fixtures.

From the choir, stairways lead down to a thirteen-by-thirty-three-foot cavern underneath the church known as the Grotto of the Nativity, presumed to be the very cave in which Jesus was born. The place of birth is marked by a low, semicircular niche of marble surrounding a polished silver star on the floor, illuminated by a collection of overornate lanterns suspended from above. Rich curtains and tapestries cascade over the sacred precinct, as well as the little adjacent niche containing a stone manger where, supposedly, the infant Jesus was laid.

Visitors are often struck by conflicting impressions. There is reverence for the holy place, certainly, and some form of Christian worship is usually taking place at the shrine, led by a Coptic, Syriac, Armenian, Greek Orthodox, or Roman Catholic priest. But there is also aesthetic disappointment: the potpourri of garish votive lanterns, icons, and candelabra which cluster about the shrine offend Western tastes. Yet this is a trifling and parochial objection, for the grotto is, after all, in the hands of Eastern Christendom.

But the dominant question in the mind of any thinking contemporary visitor to the shrine must be this: did it all really happen *here*—at this spot? Though final proof is necessarily lacking, the surprising answer lurks somewhere between "Possibly" and "Quite probably."

Where there is no direct archaeological evidence—and there could be none in the case of the birth of Jesus—nothing is more important in establishing the authenticity of an ancient site than antiquity: the place must have been regarded as such from earliest times. If the Church of the Nativity had been built here first in the year 600 A.D., for example, its claims to mark the authentic site of the birth of Jesus would be almost worthless. But Constantine the Great, the first Christian emperor of Rome, erected the original Church of the Nativity at this place in 326 A.D., over the very grotto which had been identified as the true site by the early church father Origen and before him Justin Martyr, writing in 150 A.D. They stated that Jesus was born in a cave which was used as a stable—not the typical stone or wooden stable so familiar in Christmas art. Earlier still, in the 130's, the pagan Roman emperor Hadrian tried to desecrate the Jewish and Christian holy places in Palestine, and he converted these very grotto precincts into a grove sacred to Adonis.

"How still we see thee lie. . . ."

Having hosted the birth of the individual who would change history, Bethlehem seemed content to rest on its laurels, for nothing much has happened there in the two thousand years since. One prominent exception, of course, was the sojourn of Jerome, who lived in the Church of the Nativity complex about 400 A.D. and translated parts of the Old Testament into Latin, which, with other translations, eventually became the famed Vulgate. The Vulgate has remained the official version of the Bible for Roman Catholicism ever since.

And in the modern era, it was a Syrian-Christian merchant in Bethlehem who first received the original Dead Sea Scrolls from the desert Bedouins who had discovered them in the early spring of 1947. The merchant brought them to the attention of religious authorities in Jerusalem, who alerted the entire scholarly world. Today, Bethlehem turns a brisk trade in religious items—candles, crucifixes, and sacred mementoes of olive wood and mother-of-pearl—for the many tourists from all parts of the world who throng the site where Christ was born.

Each Christmas, the town decks itself in colored lights, glass lanterns, glittering stars, and illuminated crosses, while it doubles in size because of the influx of Christian pilgrims. At twilight

Just across from the birth site in the Grotto of the Nativity stands the manger area. A stone feeding trough here is the presumed spot where Mary laid the infant Jesus.

on Christmas Eve, a Protestant carol service is conducted on a hillside at the Shepherds' Fields, and another at 9 P.M. in an outer court of the Church of the Nativity. Meanwhile, the Latin patriarch of Jerusalem leads a colorful procession from the Holy City to Bethlehem in order to conduct a midnight Mass in the Church of the Nativity, a celebration transmitted by closed-circuit television to a large screen in Manger Square for the benefit of the thousands who cannot crowd inside the basilica. At the same time, the grotto has been filled with humanity for most of Christmas Eve, as groups from all over the world read the Christmas story in a babble of foreign tongues.

Exactly at midnight, a silver bell tinkles in the grotto, heralding Christ's birthday, and many of the pilgrims are overcome as they spirit themselves back two thousand years and try to find a place between the shepherds and the Magi at the mangerside. A few move forward to try to press their lips to the metallic star marker. Then church bells peal forth throughout the city, since the people of Bethlehem are predominantly Christian.

Stone mangers of the type used in Palestine during Biblical times have been excavated at Solomon's Stables in Megiddo.

6

LOCAL SHEPHERDS, DISTANT MAGI

And in that region there were shepherds out in the field, keeping watch over their flock by night. And an angel of the Lord appeared to them, and the glory of the Lord shone around them, and they were filled with fear. And the angel said to them, "Be not afraid; for behold, I bring you good news of a great joy which will come to all the people; for to you is born this day in the city of David a Savior, who is Christ the Lord. And this will be a sign for you: you will find a babe wrapped in swaddling cloths and lying in a manger."

LUKE 2:8–12

THERE WAS SOMETHING peculiarly public about births in ancient times. There were no hospital maternity wards which only the father could visit, no looking at baby through the nursery window or breathing on him through sterile, antiseptic masks. The birth of a baby in Jewish families of the time, especially of a boy, was the signal for general rejoicing in the neighborhood and a feast for the relatives and friends, who came crowding in to see the newborn infant.

But since Joseph and Mary were in special circumstances in Bethlehem, far from their Nazareth home, festivities would be in a different key, even if they did have relatives in the Bethlehem area. Strangely, the only guests at the Nativity mentioned in the New Testament were the shepherds and the wise men.

The Herdsmen

That lowly shepherds should have been the very first to learn about what had happened in Bethlehem has struck some commentators as incongruous, and attempts have been made to "upgrade the shepherds." So they are represented as not the ordinary kind of nomadic herdsmen who often infuriated the rabbis by their manner of life, their sometimes necessary absence from the synagogue, and their failure to fulfill the Law. Instead, these were supposed to be special shepherds who were guarding flocks destined for sacrifice in the Jerusalem temple, and this would explain their readiness to welcome a newborn Messiah.

Whether or not this is true, any special "rehabilitation of the shepherds" is hardly necessary in the Christmas story. If, resorting to symbolism, the wise men represented privilege, wealth, and intelligence, so the shepherds stood for the cross-sectional, average Palestinian—quite literally, too, "the man on the night shift." For shepherding was one of the oldest and most important vocations among the ancient Hebrews, who first came into their Promised Land as nomadic shepherds and herdsmen, not farmers.

The Bible is full of references to sheep and shepherds. Such Old Testament heroes as Abraham, Isaac, Jacob, Moses, and David were all shepherds at some time in their lives, and the Twenty-third Psalm remains one of the most beautiful commentaries on shepherding ever written. In the New Testament, the familiar figure of Jesus as "The Good Shepherd" underscores the theme. In fact, the modern terms "pastor" and "bishop" both derive from the ancient words for "shepherd" and "overseer-guardian," and to this day the bishop's staff is a shepherd's crook. Perhaps it was highly appropriate after all that shepherds be the first guests at the first Christmas.

They may well have lived in the herdsmen's village of Beit Sahur, just below Bethlehem, and have been pasturing their

Religious News Service

Modern shepherds tend their sheep much like their ancient counterparts at the Shepherds' Fields just outside Bethlehem in the background.

flocks at night on the sloping expanse just east of Bethlehem which is still pointed out as the Shepherds' Fields. Besides keeping such long hours, herdsmen had to protect their sheep from ravaging animals and robbers by skillful use of staff and sling, as well as a metal-studded club about a yard long. A well-trained sheep dog was almost as effective as the shepherd in defending the flock. Herdsmen were also expected to shear the wool, aid in lambing, and see that their flock had enough to eat and drink. While the sheep were grazing, they often passed the time by playing folk tunes on their pipes.

The names of the shepherds who witnessed the Nativity will doubtless never be known, but they win our respect. Perhaps it was fortunate that they were common laymen, for had they been scholars or theologians, they would likely first have held a debate on the hillside instead of rushing into Bethlehem after the glad announcement, the conservatives insisting they would never leave the sheep, and the liberals labeling the angelic appearance a mere hallucination. No one has bothered to inquire if anyone stayed behind to watch the sheep while they were gone, but we can safely assume that the first thing the shepherds did the morning after their night of spreading word about the newborn Christ was to take a head count of their sheep!

Today, the chief breed of sheep in Palestine is the broad-tailed variety *(Ovis laticaudata),* and there is every reason to presume that the flocks still grazing in the hills around Bethlehem today descended from the very sheep whose foraging was so extraordinarily interrupted that night of nights.

The Wise Men

Now when Jesus was born in Bethlehem of Judea in the days of Herod the king, behold, wise men from the East came to Jerusalem, saying, "Where is he who has been born king of the Jews? For we have seen his star in the East and have come to worship him." (Matthew 2:1–2)

Modes of transportation and dress often seem to have changed little in Palestine during the 2,000 years since Jesus' birth. Here a Bedouin in colorful *keffiyeh*—a versatile insulation against both heat and cold—cajoles his camel.

How much time elapsed between the adoration of the shepherds and the visit of the Magi is not known, but the mysterious men from the East do not seem to have arrived until after Jesus' presentation at the Temple in Jerusalem, forty days after he was born. Unfortunately, little more is known of the Magi than of the shepherds.

"We three kings of Orient are. . . ." So the beloved Christmas carol begins, but already it has made at least three errors. First, how many wise men made the trip to Bethlehem is not known. And they were not "kings." And they did not come from as far away as the "Orient," that is, the Far East.

Tradition, of course, has placed their number at three, probably because of the three gifts of gold, frankincense, and myrrh which they presented to the infant Jesus, the assumption being one gift—one giver. But some earlier traditions make quite a caravan of their visit, setting their number as high as twelve. Legend has also supplied names in the case of the three—Gaspar, Melchior, and Balthasar—and has even reported their ages—twenty, forty, and sixty—as well as their skin colors—white, yellow, and black. But these names arise first in the sixth century A.D., too late for any authenticity, and their ages and races are too obviously spaced.

Supposedly, Thomas, the apostle to India, found and baptized the Magi into the Christian faith, ordaining them as priests. Later they suffered martyrdom, and their relics were presumably buried in Constantinople but then transferred to the cathedral at Cologne in Germany during the twelfth century, where they rest today. But no one takes such claims seriously.

The Greek of the New Testament calls them simply "*magoi apo anatolon*"—"magi from the East"—and the term *magoi* is usually translated as wise men, astrologers, or magicians. And "the East" has been variously identified as any country from Arabia to Media and Persia, but no farther east.

All the evidence points to Mesopotamian or Persian origins for the magi, who were an old and powerful priestly caste among both Medes and Persians. These priest-sages, extremely well educated for their day, were specialists in medicine, religion, astronomy, astrology, divination, and magic, and their caste eventually spread across much of the East. As in any other profession, there were both good and bad magi, depending on whether they did research in the sciences or practiced augury, necromancy, and magic. The Persian magi were credited with higher religious and intellectual attainments, while the Babylonian magi were sometimes deemed imposters.

The safest conclusion is that the Magi of Christmas were Persian, for the term originates among the Medo-Persians, and early Syriac traditions give them Persian names. Primitive Christian art in the second-century Roman catacombs dresses them in Persian garments, and a majority of early church fathers interpret them as Persian. Indeed, the reason invading Persians spared the Church of the Nativity in 614 was because they saw a golden mosaic over the doorway, depicting the wise men in Persian headdress.

On the other hand, if the astronomical aspects of the Christmas story be emphasized—the great star and its role—a case could be made that the Magi were late Babylonians, since astronomy reached its highest development in Mesopotamia.

Whatever their origin, the visit of the eastern sages was of great significance for later Christianity: the wise men were pagans, not Hebrews, and the fact that gentile magi performed the same adoration as Jewish shepherds symbolized the universal outreach for future Christianity. "And gentiles shall come to your light," the prophet Isaiah had written, "and kings to the brightness of your rising" (60:3).

The star which guided them to Bethlehem, discussed in the next chapter, had both local and international significance. The Hebrews expected a star as a sign of the birth of the Messiah (Num. 24:17)—a later pseudo-Messiah tried to capitalize on this belief by calling himself Bar-Cochba, "Son of a Star"—and eastern sages were acquainted with Hebrew beliefs because of the large Jewish colony in Babylon and elsewhere. Even Roman authors of the time spoke of the grandiose things expected in Palestine. "There had spread all over the East an old and established belief that it was fated for men coming from Judea at that time to rule the world," wrote Suetonius. Therefore when the Magi inquired of Herod, "Where is he who has been born king of the Jews?" their question was not really spoken out of a vacuum.

The scene of proud and richly costumed sages worshiping a baby in the humblest of circumstances has etched itself on the world's imagination, for it is a graphic study in contrasts. The gifts they presented are usually interpreted symbolically. Gold, a royal gift, signified Jesus' kingship. Frankincense, a fragrant gum resin burned as incense, denoted his future priesthood. This substance consisted of small whitish beads or chunks that were ground into powder and gave off an odor like balsam when burned. The third gift, myrrh, called *smyrna* in Greek, was an aromatic orange-colored resin from the small, thorny trees of the *Commiphora* family. Myrrh was expensive and much esteemed for use in perfumes, anointing oil, medicine, and embalming. That later at Calvary Jesus was offered wine mixed with myrrh as a palliative (Mk. 15:23) and was also buried with the substance (Jn. 19:39) is predictive enough.

After their adoration at the manger, the wise men disappear from history, leaving a multitude of questions in their wake. Almost unidentifiable, they have still become some of the most familiar figures in Western culture, for their clumsy camels have lumbered back into the Nativity scene every year since Christmas was first celebrated.

And they did achieve their purpose in the total story of Christmas, which was to expand it. Up to now, the Nativity had been highly local in nature: only a few people of the lower classes of just one nationality had been involved. But the visit of the Magi burst all that, as rich gentiles joined poor Jews, as King Herod and the priestly establishment in Jerusalem became concerned, and even the stars looked in.

7

AN INCREDIBLE STAR

When they had heard the king they went their way; and lo, the star which they had seen in the East went before them, till it came to rest over the place where the child was.

MATTHEW 2:9

ONE OF THE most spectacular aspects of the Christmas story must be the great star which lured the wise men from their eastern homeland to Jerusalem and on again to Bethlehem. For that star never really disappeared. In silver or gold, plastic or cardboard, it crowns the tops of Christmas trees and twinkles among the festive trappings along Main Street. In glitter or aluminum foil, it shines on as the most familiar single motif on Christmas cards.

The Star of Bethlehem has puzzled scholars for centuries. Some have skeptically dismissed the phenomenon as a myth, a mere literary device to call attention to the importance of the Nativity. Some Christians, at the other extreme, have argued that the star was miraculously placed there by God to guide the Magi and is therefore beyond all natural explanation. Most authorities, however, take a middle course which looks for some astronomical and historical explanation for the Christmas star, and several interesting theories have been offered.

First of all, there is nothing in the least improbable about a group of sages being attracted by some astral event and then trying to investigate it more closely. The ancient historians of the Near East, Greece, and Rome were fond of describing astronomical phenomena and the profound effect these had on the daily

The conjunction of Jupiter and Saturn in Pisces (the Fishes) in December of 7 B.C., as extrapolated from Babylonian records. Modern astronomical calculations place this conjunction in approximately the same position, though a few degrees farther west on the ecliptic. This is an actual photograph of the December sky over Judea, looking toward

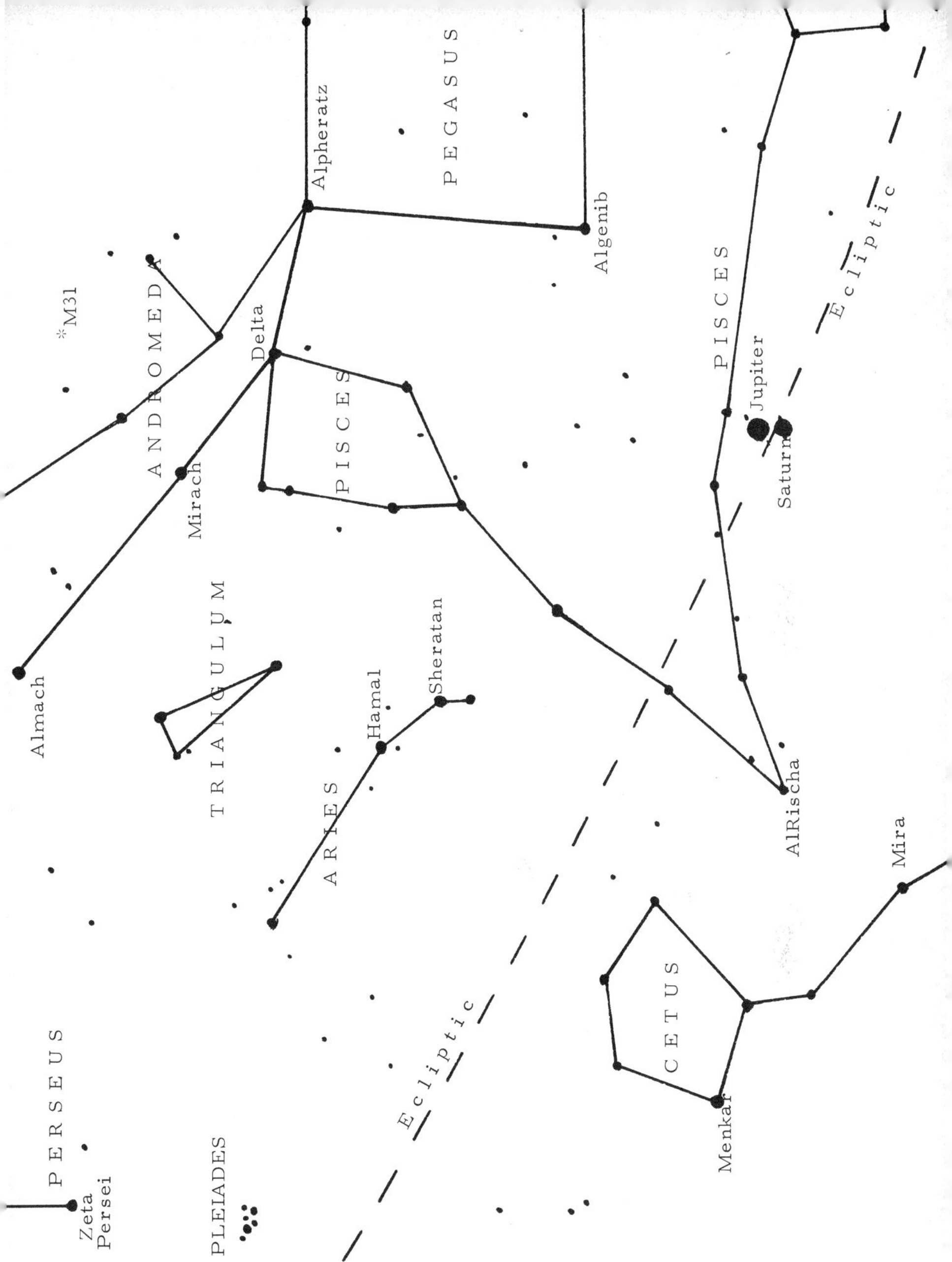

the southwest, but since a photograph is unable to reproduce the greater intensity of light from the larger planets, Jupiter and Saturn were added with enlarged diameters, as in planetariums. The constellations and stars are identified above.

lives of the people, who were forever interpreting their future on the basis of what they saw each night in the sky. In that region of clear air, and in that time of poor artificial lighting, the nights were long, and the heavens extraordinarily impressive.

From reading the historical sources, one would think comets, meteors, and other celestial wonders were almost constantly streaking across the ancient skies, and it is no accident that the present mania for astrology is traceable historically to exactly this area of the world. Indeed, the Babylonians first set up the signs of the zodiac.

There is another reason for taking the celestial event in the skies over Palestine quite seriously. If the phenomenon could be identified, astronomy could then also hope to date it, and the mystery of an exact date for the birth of Jesus would be largely solved. Here are the most logical astronomical explanations for the Star of Bethlehem.

Planetary Conjunction

Every 805 years, the planets Jupiter and Saturn come into extraordinary repeated conjunction, with Mars joining the configuration a year later. Since the great Kepler first alerted them to it in the early seventeenth century, astronomers have computed that for ten months in 7 B.C., Jupiter and Saturn traveled very close to each other in the night sky, and in May, September, and December of that year, they were conjoined. Mars joined this configuration in February of 6 B.C.—a massing of planets which must have been quite spectacular indeed. But more. The astrological interpretations of such a conjunction would have told the Magi much, if, as seems probable, they shared the astrological lore of the area. For Jupiter and Saturn met each other in that sign of the zodiac called Pisces, the Fishes.

In ancient astrology, the giant planet Jupiter was styled the "King's Planet," for it represented the highest god and ruler of the universe: Marduk to the Babylonians; Zeus to the Greeks;

Jupiter to the Romans. And the ringed planet Saturn was deemed the shield or defender of Palestine, while the constellation of the Fishes, which was also associated with Syria and Palestine, represented epochal events and crises. So Jupiter encountering Saturn in the Sign of the Fishes would have meant that a divine and cosmic ruler was to appear in Palestine at a culmination of history. This, at least, may help to explain why the Magi were well enough informed to look for some "King of the Jews" in Palestine. And the star seeming to reappear after they left Jerusalem could have been due to the planets coming back into conjunction after separating, as they did three or four times in 7–6 B.C. The time of this rare conjunction is quite possible for the birth of Jesus, though a year or two early on the basis of the most likely dating.

But there is a significant objection to this theory: the two or three planets would not have come together closely enough to represent one superstar, for they would always have been separated from each other by at least one or two moon diameters. Rather, they would have appeared as a close pair of very bright stars or a tight triangle, as in the accompanying illustration. And the triangle would have been so close to the setting sun in February of 6 B.C., that some astronomers doubt if all three planets could have been seen.

Comet

The Greek term for "star" in the Gospel account, "*aster,*" can mean any luminous heavenly body, including a comet, meteor, nova, or planet. Meteors, brief and brilliant slashes across the skies that they are, would seem too transitory for consideration. But nothing impressed the ancient eye so much as a comet, for comets were thought to herald important changes in the state, particularly by the Romans. Historians of the time report that a blood-red comet dominated the skies in the year that Caesar was assassinated, so bright that it could be seen in the daytime. A

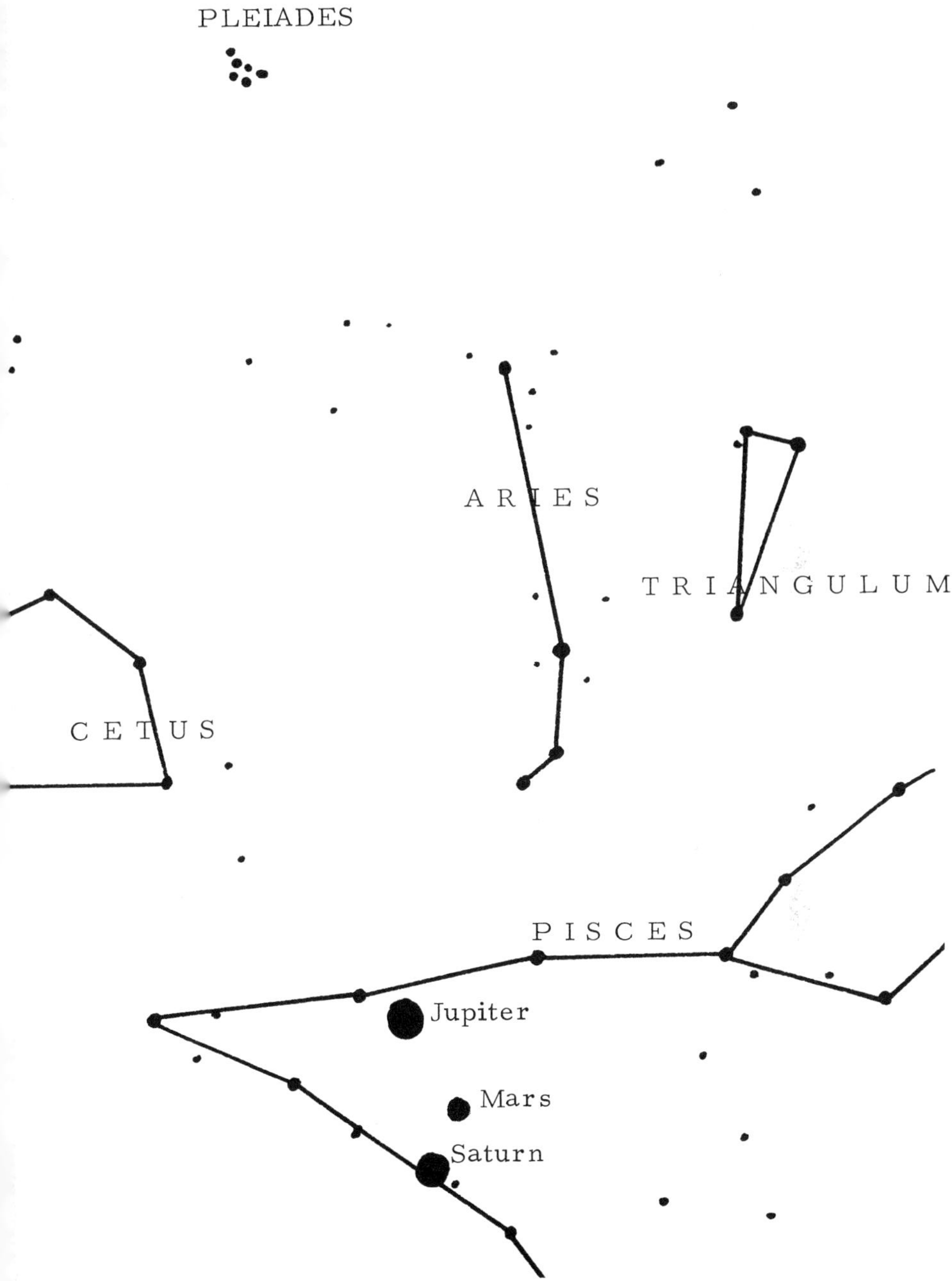

PLEIADES

ARIES

TRIANGULUM

CETUS

PISCES

Jupiter

Mars

Saturn

The massing of Jupiter, Mars, and Saturn over the western horizon in February of 6 B.C., shortly after sunset.

comet also preceded the battle of Philippi, where Caesar was avenged. The death of Augustus was also signaled by a comet, as were other political crises.

Was the Christmas star, perhaps, really a comet? With its brilliant pointing head and long luminous tail, a comet makes a far more startling impression in the night sky than any planetary conjunction. In 1910, when Halley's comet made its last pass across our neighborhood skies, Jerusalemites reported that it seemed to pass quickly from east to west, growing somewhat diffused in the east, and nearly reappearing in all its grandeur in the west, much as the phenomenon in the Nativity story. But Halley's comet passed over the skies too early (12 B.C.) in its visit at that time to be the Star of Bethlehem, although it undoubtedly aroused the interest of people in the Near East to astral events.

It happens that the Chinese have more exact and more complete astronomical records than the Near East, particularly in their tabulations of comets and novae. In 1871, John Williams published his authoritative list of comets derived from Chinese annals. Now, Comet No. 52 on the Williams list may have special significance for the first Christmas. It appeared for some seventy days in March-April of 5 B.C. near the constellation Capricorn, and would have been visible in both the Far and Near East. As each night wore on, of course, the comet would seem to have moved westward across the southern sky. The time is also very appropriate. This could indeed have been the wise men's astral marker.

Nova

A nova is not really a "new" star, as its name implies, but one that suddenly has a tremendous increase in brilliance, due to internal explosion, and no astral event is more spectacular than this. In our local galaxy of the Milky Way, the last supernova (as they are usually termed today) exploded in 1604, so brightly that it could be seen, also in daylight. The ancients sometimes con-

Comet Arend-Roland, named for the Belgians who discovered it, as photographed by the Schmidt telescope at Mount Palomar Observatory on May 1,1957.

The white arrow indicates a supernova in Galaxy NGC 4725 in the constellation Coma Berenices. Note its absence in an earlier photograph of the same sector. This supernova appeared in late 1940.

fused comets and novae, though the Chinese usually called the latter "comets without a tail."

It is quite fascinating to note that Comet No. 53 on the Williams list (next after the above) is such a tailless comet, which could well have been a nova, as Williams admitted. No. 53 appeared in March-April of 4 B.C.—a year after its predecessor—in the area of the constellation Aquila, which also was visible all over the East. Was this, perhaps, the star that reappeared to the Magi once Herod had directed them to Bethlehem (Mt. 2:9)?

The following, then, is a possible astronomical reconstruction of what happened that first Christmas. The remarkable conjunctions of Jupiter and Saturn in 7–6 B.C. alerted the Magi to important developments in Palestine, for the astrological significance closely paralleled what they had learned from Hebrew lore about a star heralding the expected Messiah. The comet of 5 B.C. (Williams No. 52) dramatically underscored this interpretation and sent them on their way, while it was the nova (or comet) of 4 B.C. (Williams No. 53) which appeared after they had reached Jerusalem and were seeking further information from Herod.

The suspicious king asked the Magi when the star first appeared, and their answer, while not given, seems indicated by Herod's massacring all male infants in Bethlehem "who were two years old or under, according to the time which he had ascertained from the wise men" (Mt. 2:16). The two years are easily explained by the difference in time between the planetary conjunction and the comets (or comet and nova), and there is no suggestion in the Christmas story that the Star of Bethlehem was shining continually during the journey of the wise men. Indeed, it seemed to have disappeared before they reached Jerusalem only to reappear as they were leaving the city.

That the star "went before them till it came to rest over the place where the child was" need not imply any sudden visible movements on the part of the astral phenomenon. Because of the rotation of the earth, anything in the night sky appears to move generally westward as the night progresses, except Polaris and the relatively few stars north of it. And, as people travel, the stars do seem to move with them or before them, stopping when they stop. So when it reached a zenith in the skies over Bethlehem, the gleaming blue-white star of Christmas would indeed have seemed to stop for the Magi as they reached their destination.

Even the artistic conceptions of the star shedding its rays down on Bethlehem might not be quite so fanciful as one would think. In subtropical latitudes on very clear nights, a faint luminous band similar to the Milky Way is visible on the southwest horizon called zodiacal light. The reflection of sunlight on meteoric particles concentrated in the plane of the ecliptic, zodiacal light appears as a luminous cone shining from the planetary path down to earth at the point where the sun has set. *If* it appeared to the Magi leaving Jerusalem, zodiacal light might have seemed to beam down from the Christmas star to intersect Bethlehem at the southwest. But this is an embellishment to the Christmas story, on which the New Testament is silent.

Perhaps this reconstruction of the astral events seems too pat to be true. Additional astronomical evidence may one day disprove it, or substantiate it after all. At least it is not so fanciful as some of the current theories. Perhaps the most grotesque is that offered by the Russian V. Zaitsev, who claims that the Star of Bethlehem was really a spaceship from a higher civilization carrying cosmonaut Jesus into this world! But beyond any (more serious) debate, astronomy does play an important role in the story of Christmas.

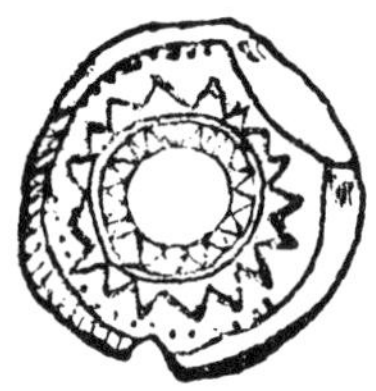

Bronze

Obv. Helmet with crest and cheek piece; inscription: ΒΑΣΙΛΕΩΣ ΗΡΩΔΟΥ (King Herod); date and monogram as below.

Rev. Circular shield, surrounded by a wavy line.

Bronze

Obv. Tripod with bowl; in field right, monogram ⳨ ; left, date: LΓ (year 3); inscription: ΒΑΣΙΛΕΩΣ ΗΡΩΔΟΥ (King Herod).

Rev. Thymiaterium (incense burner) between two palm branches.

Bronze

Obv. Anchor; inscription: BACI HPWΔ (King Herod).

Rev. Double cornucopia with caduceus between horns.

Bronze coinage of Herod the Great.

8

HEROD THE KING

Then Herod, when he saw that he had been tricked by the wise men, was in a furious rage, and he sent and killed all the male children in Bethlehem and in all that region who were two years old or under, according to the time which he had ascertained from the wise men.

MATTHEW 2:16

IT WAS ONLY NATURAL for the Magi to assume that a newborn king of the Jews would have entered this world in the royal palace at Jerusalem. But wise as they were, their inquiry before King Herod showed no great tact and even less diplomacy. "Where is he who has been born king of the Jews?" might have sounded far more courteous to the king had it been worded: "Where is the new prince who will one day succeed you?" For Herod's suspicious mind immediately warped the Magi's query into: "Where is the *real* king, you imposter?" At the time, Herod mistrusted everyone and thought himself surrounded by young aspirants all plotting to seize his throne.

Probably his first impulse was to clap the mysterious visitors into irons for asking such a question, but his native shrewdness checked it. He would have to pose interest and ferret out whatever information he could from them in order to kill off a possible rival. Instead, then, he assembled his priests and demanded to know where the Messiah-king was expected to be born. On the basis of an Old Testament prophecy, the scholars were able to pinpoint Bethlehem: "And you, O Bethlehem, in the land of Judah, are by no means least among the rulers of Judah; for from you shall come a ruler who will govern my people Israel" (Mic. 5:2; Mt. 2:6).

His eyes crinkling with suspicion even as his face wore a mask of affability, Herod directed his guests to David's city: "Go and search diligently for the child, and when you have found him bring me word, that I may come and worship him. . . ."

". . . in mockery and then kill him!" Herod's mind completed the thought.

And the wise men would have done just that but for the sudden change of plans recorded by Matthew: "Being warned in a dream not to return to Herod, they departed to their own country by another way" (2:12). Probably they headed due east into the Judean badlands, brushing just north of the Qumran wilderness community that would one day give the world the Dead Sea Scrolls. Then they crossed the Jordan River ford just above the head of the Dead Sea and returned to their eastern homeland.

Herod took that snub with all the rage of the deluded and suspicious old paranoid he had become. Ordering the ruthless massacre of all male babies two years old and under in Bethlehem and vicinity, he hoped that the infant "king" must certainly have been among the victims. Estimating a town of some 2,000 inhabitants at the time, about twenty-five male babies would have fallen into this category and been slain. The scene of mothers madly trying to hush their crying infants so as not to be discovered only to see them snatched out of their arms by Herod's soldiers, thrown to the floor, and run through with swords sends a bristle of shock into the Christmas story so utterly discordant with the rest of it. To anyone with even the slightest knowledge of the Nativity, Herod emerges quite clearly as "the monster of the Christmas story."

So incredibly brutal was this slaughter of the innocents that some scholars have superimposed a great question mark over this part of the Nativity record, suggesting that nothing of the kind ever happened. But such a crime was very much in character for Herod in his last years, when illness and court intrigue had nearly deranged the man. He married ten wives, who spawned a wriggling, ambitious brood of sons who turned the palace into a human can of worms in their scheming to succeed him.

Herod was so jealous of his favorite wife that on two occasions he ordered that she be killed if he failed to return from a critical mission. And then he finally killed her anyway, as well as her grandfather, her mother, his brother-in-law, and three of his sons, not to mention numerous subjects. During a swimming party at Jericho, he also drowned the high priest, who happened to be another of his brothers-in-law. The real villain behind many of these murders was his sister Salome, who was so jealous of Herod's wives that she sowed the seeds of suspicion for years in the Jerusalem palace, concocting monstrous lies about everyone —lies which Herod too easily believed.

Herod the Great

The young Herod, on the other hand, had been an exceptionally able ruler, governing Palestine as client-king in behalf of the Roman emperor Augustus. And the House of Herod had the uncanny knack of being able to sniff the airs of Mediterranean politics and make the right decisions. Herod's father had given crucial help to Julius Caesar when he was down in Egypt, cut off from his supplies, and Caesar rewarded him handsomely for that. Herod himself shrewdly advised his friend Mark Antony to drop Cleopatra and make peace with Rome. (Antony should have followed that advice.) And once Augustus emerged victorious from the civil wars, he was so impressed with young Herod that he allowed him to become one of his most intimate friends.

The face of Palestine was groomed and beautified during Herod's thirty-three-year reign. Across the land he erected palaces, fortresses, temples, aqueducts, cities, and—his crowning achievement—the great new Temple in Jerusalem. He created the magnificent port of Caesarea and stimulated trade and commerce. He also patronized culture in Greek cities far from Pales-

The Herodium, one of the fortresses constructed by Herod the Great, also marked his place of burial. Today the ruins of the Herodium tower over Bethlehem's southeastern horizon.

tine and easily became the talk of the eastern Mediterranean.

In fallow years or seasons of famine, Herod remitted taxes, and during one crisis he even sold his dinnerware to buy food for the populace. He also served as protector of overseas Jews in the Dispersion by conciliating their gentile rulers. He was so highly respected by Rome that he would actually go down in history as "Herod the Great."

But he had little support in his own kingdom. Herod was only a half-Jew and seemed far too Romanizing for his subjects, whom he also taxed heavily. Soon he was hated as a tyrant, even by members of his own family. A maddening maze of intrigues infested the palace, and Herod began suspecting everyone while tormented by fears of assassination. In his advancing paranoia, he was continually writing Rome for permission to execute one or two of his sons for treason. Finally even his patron and friend Augustus had to admit, "I'd rather be Herod's pig than his son." It was not only a play on the similar-sounding Greek word for son and pig, but a wry reference to the fact that pork, at least, was not consumed by Jews.

Old and very ill from arteriosclerosis, Herod worried that no one would mourn his death—a justified concern. So he issued orders from his deathbed that leaders from all parts of Judea were to be locked inside the great hippodrome at Jericho. When he died, archers were to massacre these thousands in cold blood, so there would indeed be universal mourning associated with his death.

This was the Herod at the time of the Christmas story. Would he, then, have scrupled at the lives of a few babies in little Bethlehem? Hardly! As it was, Bethlehem lay just northwest of his favorite fortress-palace, the great, breast-shaped mountain called the Herodium, where he was arranging his own tomb. Here, least of all, would he tolerate sedition in the name of any newborn "king of the Jews."

After changing his will three times and attempting suicide, Herod finally contracted a very loathsome disease in the spring of 4 B.C. which ulcerated his digestive system, inflamed his abdomen, rotted his privates, and blocked his breathing. After a last, fevered convulsion, he died.

But alas, Herod's final plans—both of them—miscarried. The Jewish leaders who were jammed inside the hippodrome were not slaughtered but released. And the baby who was supposed to die in the Bethlehem massacre was instead jogging in the arms of his mother as she sat astride a donkey en route to refuge in Egypt.

The Journeys of the First Christmas

9

UP TO JERUSALEM, DOWN TO EGYPT

And at the end of eight days, when he was circumcised, he was called Jesus, the name given by the angel before he was conceived in the womb. —And when the time came for their purification according to the law of Moses, they brought him up to Jerusalem to present him to the Lord.

LUKE 2:21–22

TRAVEL IS as typical of the modern yuletide as the blazing Christmas tree itself. In our mobile society, highways and airlines are crowded each December as younger members of the family come home for Christmas and relatives get together for the holidays. What other society has nearly made a carol out of "I'll be Home for Christmas"?

Travel also characterized the first Christmas. Besides Joseph and Mary's tedious journey from Galilee to Bethlehem, there was the immense westward trek of the wise men across hundreds of miles of desert to Judea and back again. Then too, soon after the Nativity, the Holy Family took three important trips, two in order to fulfill Jewish religious law, and the third to save the very life of the newborn child.

The Circumcision

On the eighth day after he was born, every Hebrew boy baby was circumcised, a token of the special covenant between God and his chosen people dating back to Abraham (Gen. 17:10 ff.).

At this ceremony, the child was also formally given his name. The rite became one of the most important hallmarks of Judaism, and some of their savants even claimed that the higher angels were created in a circumcised condition.

Under normal circumstances, the nearest rabbi would have come to the home of Joseph and Mary to perform the ceremony, but since they may still have been living in the grotto, or more likely in a rented dwelling at Bethlehem, they probably took the infant to a nearby synagogue for the all-important rite. Presumably, Joseph asked the rabbi to let him help officiate, a common request in these happy circumstances, and the rabbi cheerfully agreed.

However it happened, the circumcision-naming ceremony was an occasion for great joy among parents, relatives, and friends, with many overtones of the later Christian baptism. In Jesus' case, probably only Joseph, Mary, and the nameless rabbi shared the gladness that another son of Israel had been included in the great covenant with God. And the baby was given a proper Scriptural name, that of Moses' successor as leader of the Hebrews: Joshua or Yeshua. It meant "God saves" or "God is salvation." Later ages would prefer the Greek form of the name, Jesus.

For some days after circumcision, the baby would be uncomfortable, the first token pain and bloodshed in a career that would see considerably more of both.

The Presentation at the Temple

After forty days it was time for Jesus' first longer journey. Moses' law required that women had to purify themselves after childbirth by offerings at the Tabernacle (or, later, Temple) forty days after the birth of a boy, and eighty after that of a girl. It was a simple, six-mile trip north to Jerusalem, doubtless on the same patient little jackass that had carried Mary down to Bethlehem, and it should not have taken more than two hours.

The magnificent Temple in Jerusalem was approaching completion at the time, a gleaming white jewel wedged into the northeastern corner of the city. The sprawling enclave was rimmed with a labyrinth of colonnaded porticoes and gates, and to all pious Jews this was the very center of the world. What Joseph and Mary offered for her purification showed how poor they were, for in lieu of sacrificing an unblemished yearling lamb, they offered instead a pair of turtledoves or pigeons (Lev. 12), the minimum requirement of religious law.

At the same time they also formally presented the infant Jesus back to God in fulfillment of Exodus 13:2 ("Dedicate to me every first-born . . ."), redeeming or buying him back again through an offering of five silver shekels, about $3.25 (Num. 18:16). This shows, incidentally, that Jesus was free of any bodily blemish or this ceremony would not have been necessary.

Everything had happened normally enough up to that moment. But then, as Joseph and Mary were standing with their bundled infant in the Court of the Women at the great Temple, a righteous and devout old man named Simeon walked purposefully over to them with a strange glint in his eye. For years he had been waiting for the fulfillment of messianic expectations, he explained to the awestruck couple, and God had assured him that he would indeed live to see the infant Christ. That very morning he had been inspired to come into the Temple and view the culmination of his hopes. Exuberantly taking the baby in his arms, old Simeon exulted:

> Lord, now lettest thou thy servant depart in peace,
> according to thy word;
> for mine eyes have seen thy salvation
> which thou hast prepared in the presence of all peoples,
> a light for revelation to the Gentiles,
> and for glory to thy people Israel.
>
> (Luke 2:29–32)

The words would ring down in Christian history as one of the most beloved prayers of the church, and artists would never tire of trying to catch on canvas the sacred fire in Simeon's eyes.

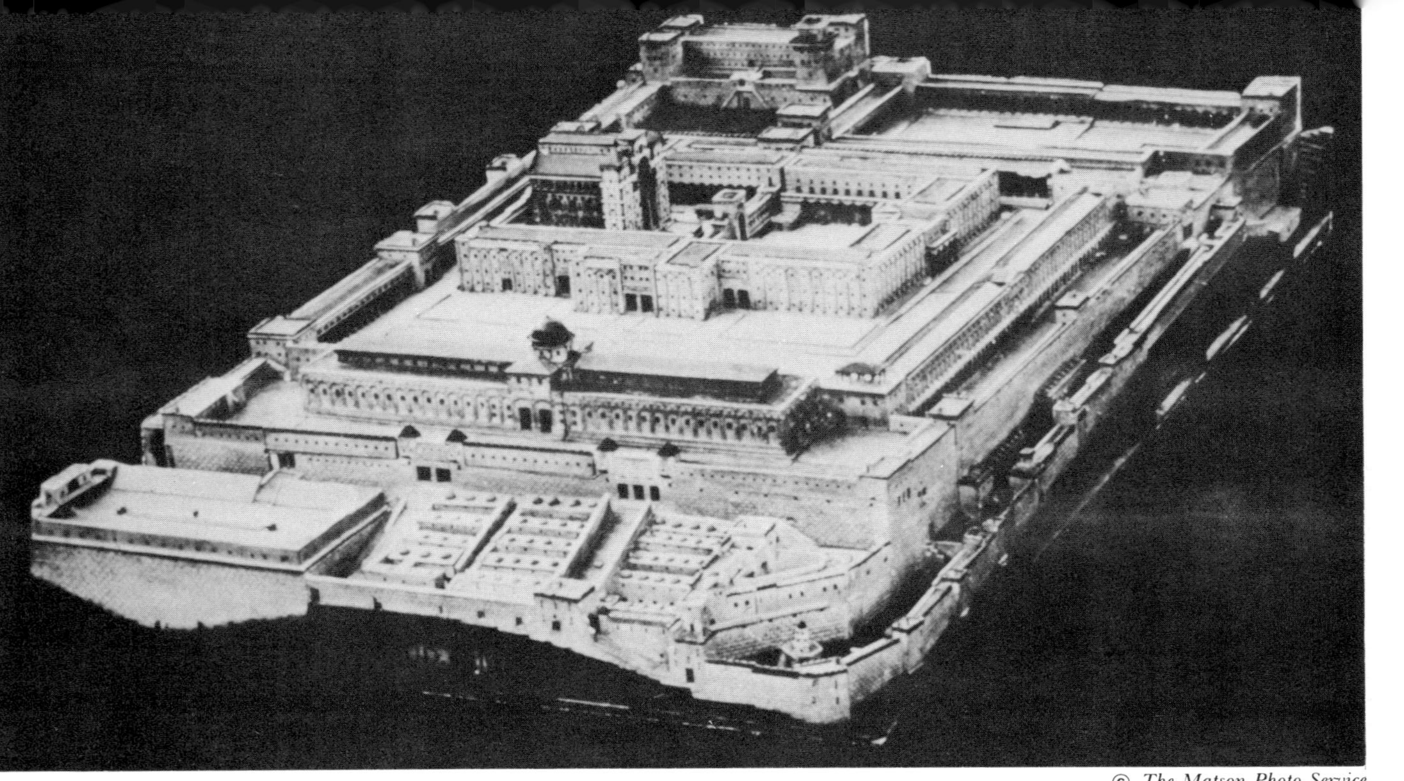

Reconstruction of the great Temple in Jerusalem, built by Herod the Great, where the infant Jesus was presented. In the upper left center is the Holy of Holies. (This model was designed by scholar-engineer Dr. Conrad Schick.)

Then he turned to Joseph and Mary and blessed them, adding some prophetic words: "Behold, this child is set for the fall and rising of many in Israel, and for a sign that is spoken against. . . ." And so Simeon had played out his role as a transition figure, the man, more than any other, who stands between the Old and New Testaments, rooted in the ancient Scriptural promises and prophecies, yet gazing at their fulfillment.

Old as Simeon looked, his face almost took on the bloom of youth compared with the decrepit figure who now hobbled over to them, her leather skin mottled with bleached or browned patches and deeply latticed with wrinkles. Her name was Anna, her role was that of prophetess, and she had been a human fixture at the Temple for most of her incredible life-span. She was either eighty-four or about one hundred and six years old, since Luke's language is not explicit. Anna came from the tribe of Asher—clearly, the so-called "Ten Lost Tribes" of Israel had not lost all their members—and she formed the perfect female counterpart to Simeon, thanking God and immediately telling others of the wonder that had happened in the form of the six-week-old Jesus.

The Flight to Egypt

> Now when [the wise men] had departed, behold, an angel of the Lord appeared to Joseph in a dream and said, "Rise, take the child and his mother, and flee to Egypt, and remain there till I tell you; for Herod is about to search for the child, to destroy him." (Matthew 2:13)

Shortly after Joseph and Mary returned to Bethlehem at the close of their astonishing day at the Temple, their sense of wonder was only compounded by the visit of the Magi. But the brimming happiness of the first Christmas was abruptly cut short by what was more properly Joseph's nightmare than his dream, alerting him to Herod's designs on Jesus. Without even waiting for the morning light, Joseph roused his sleeping family, packed the drowsy, dumfounded donkey, and they all set out on the highway south toward Hebron. The journey down to Egypt

NASA

Panorama of Egypt, the Red Sea, the Sinai peninsula, Palestine (upper center) and across the Arabian desert to the Euphrates River valley (extreme upper right), taken by the Gemini 11 mission with astronauts Conrad and Gordon in September, 1966. The dotted line indicates the most likely route taken by the Holy Family on the Flight to Egypt.

The great pyramids and sphinx at Gizeh, near Cairo, which had already been standing some 2,500 years by the time the Holy Family reached Egypt.

would be far more ambitious than that which led from Nazareth to Bethlehem, well over twice as long.

The New Testament tells us nothing about the route they took, but the regular caravan trail from Bethlehem led south on the Hebron road, then sharply west to Gaza and the coastal highway down to Pelusium, the portal to Egypt. An alternate route lay in the desert interior, but it would have been extremely dangerous for a lone couple and baby to try to brave the howling sands of the northern Sinai. With an average twenty miles per day of fairly level travel along the coastal route, the Holy Family would reach Egypt in about ten days.

Wherever the Bible is silent, legend is highly vocal. And so the apocryphal *Arabic Gospel of the Infancy* tries to fill in the details of the Flight to Egypt. One of its delightful stories tells how Joseph and Mary were waylaid by robbers on the Sinai road, but they found nothing to steal from the poor couple. Taking pity on them instead, the bandits gave them provisions and sent them on their way. One of these likable brigands, of course, would cross Jesus' path thirty years later at the Crucifixion. Who but the penitent thief on his right?

There were many kindred Jews living in Egypt at the time with whom Joseph and Mary could have sought refuge. In fact, more Jews lived in Alexandria than in Jerusalem, forming 40 per cent of the population there. But it seems unlikely that the Holy Family would have traveled that far west in the Nile delta. Their place of sojourn in Egypt is unknown, although two late traditions have tried to identify it.

Near the ruins of Heliopolis, outside of Cairo, the so-called "Tree of Mary" drew pilgrims as early as the fifth century, a spreading sycamore under which Mary is supposed to have shaded herself. And in the Coptic quarter of Old Cairo stands the church of St. Sergius, below which is a crypt venerated from the sixth century as the place where the Holy Family stayed for three months while in Egypt. The crypt was originally a cave or grotto, and visitors are still shown a niche in the wall where the baby Jesus is supposed to have slept.

Wherever they stayed, it could not have been for long, since King Herod died soon after Joseph and Mary had fled from Bethlehem. Matthew finishes his version of the Christmas story by telling of another angelic dream in which Joseph is alerted to Herod's demise and told to return to Palestine, fulfilling the prophecy: "Out of Egypt have I called my son" (Hos. 11:1).

When Joseph and Mary returned to their homeland, an unhappy surprise awaited them. Herod was indeed dead, but his son Archelaus ruled Judea as his successor, and he had begun his reign with a massacre of three thousand Jews who had rebelled against him in the Temple at Jerusalem. Better to return home to Galilee, they decided, where a milder son of Herod named Antipas had been appointed tetrarch, with the kind permission of the Roman emperor Augustus.

The Foster Father of the First Christmas

10

JOSEPH THE CARPENTER

"Is not this the carpenter's son? Is not his mother called Mary?"

MATTHEW 13:55

THE FOCAL POINT of any Nativity scene or of any crèche under the Christmas tree lies just over the heads of the adoring shepherds and wise men. It is a husband and wife flanking a manger, looking down on the Child with a magnificent mixture of joy and wonder.

Joseph and Mary would become history's most famous couple because of the all but incredible circumstances. Mary was the baby's mother, but Joseph served only as its foster father, according to Christian theology, with God himself the true father. (Liberal theologians, however, and non-Christians generally deny the Virgin Birth.) If Joseph himself harbored any human misgivings about the extraordinary role his wife had been called upon to play, they are not recorded in the New Testament. Nor is there any hint that he chafed at not being able to assert his marital rights before the birth of Jesus, which would have been easy grounds for divorce in the courts today.

There are very few glimpses of Joseph in the Bible, and most of these are tied in with the Christmas story. Here the attractive figure of a considerate, protective, mature individual—a truly good man—playing his difficult role obediently and well is unmistakable. He did not resent the intrusion of shepherds and Magi but rejoiced with them in the birth of a son whom they all believed to be the long-awaited Messiah-king. A pious Jew, he saw to it that the circumcision and presentation of the infant Jesus went according to Old Testament schedule. A good provider and defender, he managed the lengthy trips to and from Egypt with no recorded difficulty—hardly a mean accomplishment for desert travel. By any measure, the noble Joseph is the unsung hero of the Christmas story.

The Craftsman

Up in Nazareth he was known as Joseph the Carpenter. And like the famous patriarch Joseph for whom he was named, he too seems to have had a father named Jacob, of whom nothing is known save that he was son of Matthan, and so on up the famous genealogy given at the beginning of Matthew's gospel.

Joseph may also have been born in Bethlehem, since his ancestors lived there, and this is where he came to register for the Roman census. But why, in that case, had he moved up to Nazareth? Perhaps it was economic competition from Bethlehem's too plentiful supply of craftsmen, or it may have been some construction project in Galilee which drew him north. It seems he was not planning to live there permanently, for after the Flight to Egypt, Joseph was thinking of returning to Bethlehem. It was only when he learned that Herod's son Archelaus ruled in Judea that he was frightened away from the land and turned back to Nazareth. The Galilean village would take on fresh importance now, since Sepphoris, which had overshadowed it, had just been destroyed because it had served as headquarters for Judas, a Galilean rebel. Then too, with most of her family in Galilee, Mary was doubtless just as happy.

After that, the obedient Joseph almost drops out of recorded history. Twelve years later comes a final glance at him in the role of a puzzled parent, wondering what had become of his prodigy-son during a trip to Jerusalem for the Passover festival. At the time, the almost-teenage Jesus was holding theological discussions with savants in the Temple, but he quickly returned with his parents to Nazareth and was obedient to them.

After giving Jesus a normal upbringing, Joseph started training him to be an apprentice carpenter, for later Jesus could even be called a "carpenter" as such. In a revealing passage in Mark's record, the Galileans, amazed at Jesus' teachings, asked: "Where did this man get all this? . . . Is not this the carpenter, the son of Mary?" (6:2–3). The apocryphal *Gospel of Thomas* tells several charming stories of Jesus at work in the carpenter shop, miraculously extending the length of several beams that Joseph had not cut to proper size.

But after this, nothing more is heard of Joseph. At no time does he appear again during the three-year public ministry of Jesus, and the safest assumption is that he had died in the meantime. His wife Mary, on the other hand, emerges at several important incidents in Jesus' career, including the Crucifixion, for which Joseph would certainly have been present had he been alive.

Another important, but overlooked, clue that Joseph did not live to see the culmination of Jesus' career comes from the Christmas record itself. When Joseph and Mary were presenting the infant Christ at the Temple, the aged Simeon turned only to Mary when he prophesied, "And a sword will pierce through your own soul also," indicating the sorrows of Calvary would affect Mary, but not Joseph. Luke, who certainly wrote his gospel after the death of Joseph, saw no reason to adjust that prediction but simply related it (2:35).

Again, however, tradition and legend have exuberantly sketched in the areas left blank by the New Testament writings. The *Protevangelium of James* and the *History of Joseph the Carpenter,* both apocryphal works of the second and fourth century respectively, portray Joseph as a widower with children when he became engaged to Mary, who was presumably only twelve years old at the time. Joseph himself worked in the timber yards of Galilee, in these sources, and also made tabernacles along the Sea of Galilee. Supposedly, he died at the ripe old age of one hundred and eleven. Needless to say, these traditions have little value.

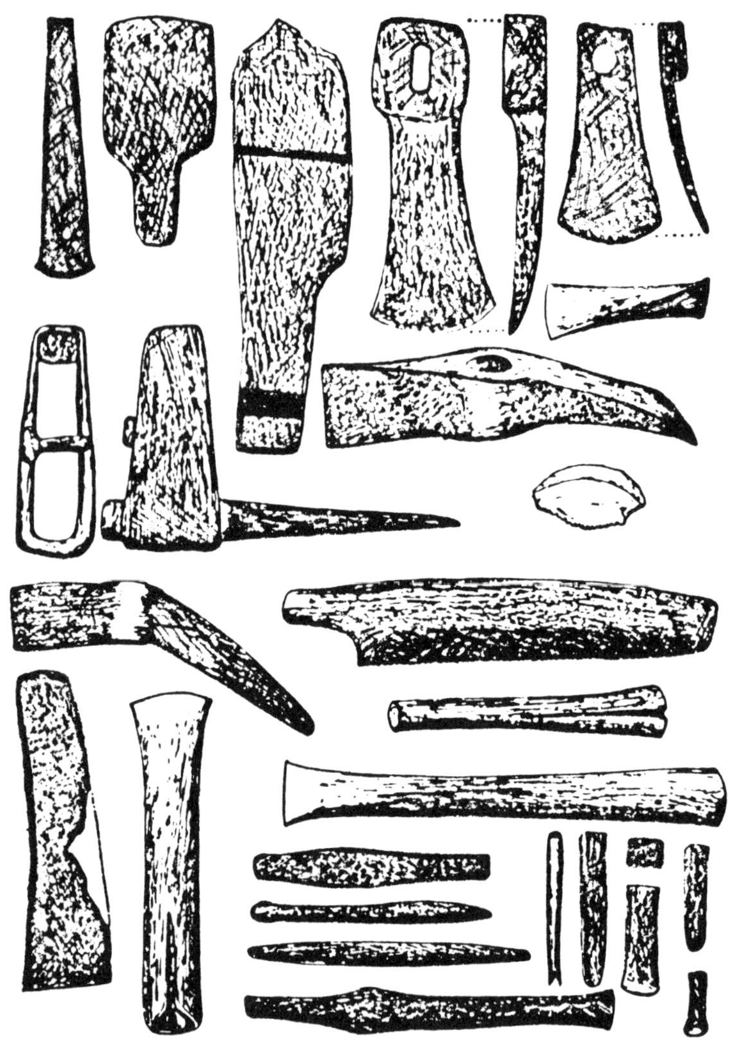

Palestine Exploration Fund

Palestinian carpenter's tools, discovered in archaeological excavations at Gezer.

Other Children?

But this does raise the question of whether or not Joseph and Mary had children after the birth of Jesus and were an otherwise normal family. The evidence is much disputed. Several passages in the New Testament seem to provide an obvious answer, for they do indeed mention brothers and sisters of Jesus. For example, here is the full reaction of the Galileans at the start of Jesus' public ministry: "Is not this the carpenter, the son of Mary and brother of James and Joses and Judas and Simon, and are not his sisters here with us?" (Mk. 6:3). The identical listing is repeated in Matthew 13:55, with the exception of "Joseph" for "Joses." The names of the sisters are not given anywhere in the New Testament, though the apocryphal *History of Joseph* calls them Anna and Lydia.

The Protestant interpretation, generally, is to take the passages at face value and reply: Yes, Jesus did indeed have half-brothers and half-sisters, and these are their names, at least in the case of the men. Matthew's statement that Joseph engaged in no marital privileges with Mary "until she had borne a son" (1:25) is often cited to support this interpretation, as is Luke's assertion that she gave birth to "her *first*-born son" (2:7).

At first these brothers were indifferent to, or critical of, Jesus (Jn. 7:5), but after the Crucifixion, they became active Christians and leaders of the early church (Acts 1:14). James became the patriarch of the Christian church in Jerusalem, and Judas presumably wrote the epistle of Jude in the New Testament.

On the other hand, Roman Catholicism, Eastern Orthodoxy, and some Protestants affirm the perpetual virginity of Mary, and identify the brothers and sisters above either as children of Joseph by a prior marriage, or the children of Mary, wife of Alphaeus, who was the sister of the Virgin Mary and thus Jesus' cousins. The term "brother" is usually used in the New Testament in the literal sense, but sometimes may indicate cousins, close relatives, and friends.

Christendom has lived very comfortably with either interpretation, even while theologians continue to debate the issue. The New Testament has the happy habit of being a little less than explicit in areas that do not pertain to the core of the faith.

11

MARY THE VIRGIN

And Mary said, "My soul magnifies the Lord, and my spirit rejoices in God my Savior, for he has regarded the low estate of his handmaiden."

LUKE 1:46–48

WHETHER OR NOT she had other children after Jesus, Mary occupies a wholly unique place in the history of religion. All three major branches of Christianity—Roman Catholicism, Protestantism, and Eastern Orthodoxy—agree with Mary's own prediction in *The Magnificat.* Because of her extraordinary role in bearing Jesus, she said, "henceforth all generations will call me blessed" (Lk. 1:48). And they have done just that, in painting, carving, sculpture, hymnody, verse, prose, prayer, and whatever other media can communicate human feeling.

It was a simple Galilean girl who made so apparently extravagant a prediction. Critics may claim that the author of the Third Gospel put the words in her mouth, but even if that were true the statement continues to amaze, since these words were first written down about 70 A.D., at a time when the tiny Christian church was undergoing what seemed a bloody and terminal persecution. And yet Mary is recorded as saying that all future generations would know of her role in the Christmas event, which is exactly what happened in fact!

The little fourteen- or fifteen-year-old Jewess was called by an alternate form of the name of Moses' sister Miriam. Mary meant, approximately, "the Lord's beloved" and it was as common in

Palestine at the time as it is today. She was undoubtedly of Davidic descent, while a very early tradition identifies her parents as Joachim and Anna.

This source, the *Protevangelium of James,* is an apocryphal work of the second century A.D., which was the first to sketch in so many of the details missing in the pre-Christmas story about Mary. It tells charmingly of the pious Joachim and Anna who had been married for many years, but without any offspring—a humiliating sorrow for them both. The wealthy old couple prayed so fervently for a child that an angel finally announced to each separately that they would have a daughter.

After Mary was born, so the *Protevangelium* continues, Joachim and Anna gratefully dedicated her when she was only three years old to a life of service at the Temple. Little Mary eagerly skipped up the fifteen steps at the gate of the Temple and, without so much as a backward glance at her parents, she remained there until she was twelve years old "like a dove that dwelt there, and she received food from the hand of an angel."

Later, she and six other virgins were given the task of weaving a new scarlet and purple curtain for the Temple, and it was while she was engaged in this work that the angelic Annunciation took place. But when her pregnancy was discovered, Mary and her elderly protector-betrothed Joseph were brought before the high priest, protesting their innocence. Both were forced to undergo the water test for adultery, which would have caused a miscarriage according to Old Testament law (Num. 5:16 ff.). But they passed the ordeal successfully.

Finally, the apocryphon has its own version of the events in Bethlehem. It tells of Joseph searching for a midwife while Mary took shelter in a cave. As the midwife approached the cavern with Joseph, a great cloud obscured it and then an intense light appeared. The clouds broke to reveal the newborn infant, nursing at Mary's breast.

These are charming additions to the Christmas story, but are they reliable or historical? While so early a source as the second-

Mary's Well in Nazareth (sometimes called The Virgin's Fountain), a natural spring which has flowed for centuries and may well have been the place where Mary drew water for her household. The women of Nazareth usually gather here in the evenings, filling large earthen jugs with the day's water supply.

"Here the Word was made flesh"—the Latin lettering reads—in a crypt below the altar in the Church of the Annunciation in Nazareth.

century *Protevangelium* must command a good deal of respect, the document was proscribed as heretical by the very earliest papal *Index,* and its embellishments, however picturesque, are not accepted as authentic today.

The Sites in Nazareth

Sometimes archaeology can supply hard evidence in place of the flimsies of literary fantasy, and efforts have been made to locate Mary's childhood home in Nazareth, as well as the house she later shared with Joseph and Jesus. But the results are much disputed.

Today, to be sure, visitors are shown the Church of the Annunciation, the largest Christian sanctuary in the Near East, constructed over the rockhewn Grotto of the Annunciation, where Mary presumably lived and was greeted by the angel. Eloquent Latin words still identify the mystery of the Incarnation in metal lettering over the base of the altar erected there: "VERBUM CARO HIC FACTUM EST'"—"Here the Word was Made Flesh."

Some distance north of the Church of the Annunciation stands the Church of St. Joseph, so named because it is commonly believed to shelter the house and workshop of Mary and Joseph in its crypt, the place where Jesus spent his boyhood. And west of it is a chapel supposedly built over the synagogue where Jesus gave his first public address in his home town (Lk. 4:16 ff.). Even the fountain or well where Mary drew her water has been marked by an adjacent chapel, the Church of St. Gabriel, where Eastern Orthodoxy believes the Annunciation took place.

But are these sites authentic? Unfortunately, the identifications are rather precarious, because the task of locating the true sites has been severely complicated by the fact that Christian shrines were not erected here until well into the fourth century A.D., and they were later devastated by Muslim attacks. Since there is only one natural spring in Nazareth, however, the Well of Mary is undoubtedly authentic, and water seems to have been drawn from it for two millennia and more. Today, Nazareth is the largest Christian city in Israel, and also contains its largest Arab population.

Mary's Later Life

Unlike Joseph, Mary appears at several important episodes in her son's public ministry, and her various vignettes in the New Testament show a woman of much spiritual sensitivity, loyalty, and concern, even at times when she, like the disciples, did not always seem to understand the fathomless depths of Jesus' mission. Yet even at the tragedy of Calvary she stood as the grieving but submissive model of all that was finest in Jewish motherhood, as Jesus commended her into the care of his disciple John.

After the New Testament accounts of Christ's death and resurrection, a new fulfillment brightened Mary's life as she finally plumbed the whole dimension of Jesus' renewed existence, and she was closely associated with the disciples in the founding of the Jerusalem church. From this point on, history breaks off, and various early traditions have Mary accompanying John to Asia Minor, or remaining in Judea. One legend tells of her spending the rest of her days in Ephesus and finally dying there, while another has her death and assumption in Jerusalem, as witnessed by the apostles who had been miraculously reassembled.

Because of her absolutely unique role in bearing the man whom Christians call the Son of God, two thousand years of theology would further explore Mary's role, culminating in 1854 when Roman Catholicism officially defined her as both sinless and immaculately conceived, and in 1950 when it declared her bodily assumption into heaven. Protestants, however, deny these dogmas because of lack of New Testament evidence.

The most familiar view of Mary, however, is the Mary of Christmas, rejoicing not only in the natural experience of motherhood, but in reverent awe at the extraordinary son she had brought into the world. There would be sorrow ahead—not just the rigorous journey into Egypt but the future fact of Calvary. Yet, for the present, Mary would rejoice.

And she also had enough presence of mind to serve as historian for the exceptional event in the absence of any historians: "But Mary kept all these things, pondering them in her heart" (Lk. 2:19). According to earliest church tradition, it was Mary herself who told Luke all about the Nativity, and it was he who wrote it down. And that is how we got the story of the first Christmas.

12

JESUS OF NAZARETH

. . . They returned into Galilee, to their own city, Nazareth. And the child grew and became strong, filled with wisdom; and the favor of God was upon him.

LUKE 2:39–40

THE BABY is what it was all about. If he had not grown up to become the Jesus Christ of the New Testament, we would never even have heard of the story of Christmas, despite its beauty, simplicity, and wonder. But something began at the Nativity which has never ended. The infant would change history, wrench the world's chronology so that its years would pivot about his birth, and touch countries, cultures, civilizations, and untold millions of lives.

Whenever those strange public-opinion polls are repeatedly taken, asking, "Who is the most admired man in history?" Jesus of Nazareth has no trouble vastly outdistancing Winston Churchill, the current favorite runner-up. However the child of Christmas be regarded, Son of God or merely mortal man, there is no question that this life affected the future more than that of any other human being who ever lived. For the Christianity which he founded has become the most successful single phenomenon in the history of the world: no other religion, philosophy, way of life, nation, or cause has commanded the loyalties of over 800,000,000 people—in the present generation alone—and none is so widespread.

The supreme paradox must be this: the person behind this

achievement taught publicly for only three and one-half years. He wrote no book. He had no powerful religious or political machine behind him—indeed, the ranking spiritual and governmental authorities opposed him—and yet he became the central figure in human history.

The Book about him now has a billion copies in print in a thousand languages, and yet no one even wrote his biography in our sense of the term, since the four accounts of him given in the Gospels offer detail only on the two extremities of his life: his birth, and his last three years. Of the some thirty intervening years, we know next to nothing. The only reported episode happened when Joseph and Mary took the twelve-year-old Jesus along with them to Jerusalem for their annual Passover festival visit, but then lost him in the Holy City. Their astonishment at finding the lad sitting among the scholars in the Temple, amazing them by his intellectual expertise, is as familiar as the Nativity story itself.

The Hidden Years

The Gospels were never intended as full biographies in the modern sense, but rather as records of Jesus' public ministry. They focus, then, not on the thirty "hidden years," as they are called, when he grew to manhood and prepared his mission, but on the all-important forty-two months when he came out of obscurity. Only then was he finally old enough to be listened to by his countrymen, who never really trusted anyone *under* thirty in matters religious.

But Jesus was a human being—and humans love childhood stories—so, once again, the apocryphal gospels were only too happy to supply them. Several of the anecdotes are pleasant enough. When he was a three-year-old toddler, Jesus took a dried fish, put it in a basin of water, and ordered it to shed its salt and come back to life. The fish, of course, did just that, swimming happily about. Several years later, Jesus was out playing with some neighborhood boys, and he made twelve model sparrows out of clay. When he clapped his hands, the birds came to life, and they flew away chirping. Then there was the time two great snakes slithered out of a cave, sending his playmates running off screaming. But Jesus calmly ordered the creatures to prostrate themselves at Mary's feet, which they promptly did.

He had no trouble getting down from precarious perches. Once while he was playing on a roof in Nazareth—obviously Mary was not around at the time—Jesus simply grabbed onto a shaft of sunlight and slid down on it to the ground. Other stories tell of his healing people long before his teens, and even raising one of his chums named Zeno from the dead.

But the other apocryphal childhood tales are not so charming, like that of the schoolmaster who tried to punish the precocious Jesus but found his hand withering instead. In some of the stories, Jesus appears as an almighty urchin—a dangerous enough combination—with no control over his cruel and childish caprice. So one of his playmates who accidentally hit Jesus in the shoulder falls over dead when Jesus curses him, and the parents of the stricken child beg Joseph to take Jesus away "or at least teach him to bless and not to curse." When Joseph reprimanded Jesus and twisted his ear, the lad warned, "I am not thine. Vex me not."

Another playmate, who offended Jesus less, was merely changed into a ram. And vice versa: once, when Jesus rode a mule, the animal was released from some magical curse and turned back into a fine young man.

Needless to say, each of these puerile stories has as much validity as a fairy tale and as much substance as a fantasy. One wonders why Medieval artists were so impressed with them as themes for their canvas and stained glass. The Fourth Gospel is clear in suggesting that Jesus' first miracle did not take place until he was an adult at the Galilean marriage in Cana (Jn. 2:11).

An Apprentice Carpenter

These may have become years of silence for subsequent ages, but they were normal enough for the child Jesus. Some missing pieces of the picture-puzzle of his youth can easily be carved to fit. His schooling, for example, was probably no different from that of the other village children in Nazareth. His first lessons, inevitably, came from Mary. But when he was about five, Jesus, like other Jewish children of the time, received much of his primary education at the synagogue, where he and the other pupils sat on the floor about the *hassan* or teacher, repeating verses from the Torah until they knew them by heart. Jesus could read and write both Aramaic and Hebrew, and he undoubtedly knew common Greek as well, for he seems to have had no trouble conversing with the Syrophoenician woman or Pontius Pilate. A few Latin words are sprinkled in his vocabulary as well.

He also had to learn a trade of some kind, for it was a rule among the Jews that every man had to work with his hands, even those destined for a religious profession. "Whoever fails to teach his son a craft teaches him to steal" was a rabbinical maxim. The great Rabbi Hillel was a woodcutter, the later apostle Paul of Tarsus a tentmaker, and Jesus of Nazareth a carpenter, like his foster father. In Jesus' case there was probably the added necessity of learning a craft to supplement the family's meager income.

The early church father Justin Martyr, born in Samaria around 100 A.D., wrote that Joseph and Jesus specialized in plows and yokes in their carpenter shop. They were of excellent durable quality, Justin claimed, and some of them were still in use in the mid-second century.

Carpenters of the time also constructed beds, boxes, coffins, benches, stools, troughs, and threshing boards, as well as more elaborate projects like boats and houses. Though the first floor of nearly all homes in Nazareth would be cut out of the soft limestone of the hill in which the town is situated, or built of stone blocks, the upper stories of larger houses were made of wood. The bronze and iron tools the carpenters used have been found in excavations at Galilee and elsewhere, and some of them have a familiar, almost modern, design. Only the power tools, it seems, are missing. And wooden joints were mitered, mortised, or dovetailed in the same configurations learned in any high school shop classes today.

There were also specialist carpenters who did inlay work and even carved artificial teeth. Skilled carpentry was late in arriving in Palestine, for David had to import Tyrian carpenters to build his palace, and Solomon his temple, while Ezra had to bring in Phoenician craftsmen even to repair it.

Images at Maturity

One old tradition, the *History of Joseph the Carpenter,* has Jesus a nineteen-year-old when Joseph died. This is very possible. In that case, Joseph would have been nearly fifty years old at his death—if he married between twenty-five and thrity—which was about the average life expectancy for the time, though many lived longer.

Jesus was now a man—a man who has been the subject of more books than any other person in history. But, apart from the many familiar accounts of his extraordinary ministry, what was he really like?

His physical appearance is not certain. Because of the famous Hebrew restriction against idolatry—"You shall not make yourself a graven image, or any likeness of anything . . ." (Ex. 20:4)—art suffered among the Jews, and the earliest representations of Jesus are not Palestinian but Roman. In the Christian catacombs, he is pictured as a beardless Roman youth tending sheep, though in fact he probably wore a trimmed beard in the style of his fellow Galileans.

The earliest bronze statue of Jesus could well have been authentic, for the church historian Eusebius himself saw it in the gentile city of Caesarea Philippi near the base of Mt. Hermon. It was said to have been erected by the woman whom Jesus healed of a chronic hemorrhage (Mk. 5:25 ff.), and it showed her resting on one knee in the position of a suppliant before the figure of Christ, who wore "a double cloak neatly draped over his shoulders with his hand stretched out to the woman." But this statue was destroyed by the emperor Julian "the Apostate." Luke, a gentile Greek, is supposed to have painted likenesses of Jesus, Peter, and Paul, but no trace of these has been found.

Jesus' physical appearance must have seemed very normal indeed—no towering figure, no nimbus, no halo. His enemies required the services of a Judas to point him out in the dusk of Jerusalem, Mary Magdalene mistook him for a gardener at the Easter tomb, and to the Emmaus disciples he looked like nothing more than a fellow traveler.

Yet he must have been an arresting figure of great intellect and much oratorical ability—persuasive, attractive, impressive. Crowds could listen to him for hours, since he spoke with authority. To his enemies, on the other hand, he appeared as a deceiver, a blasphemer, a false prophet. The response to Jesus, then, was hardly ever neutral. He captured the people or antagonized them.

He was no ascetic: he enjoyed a good time, provided party supplies on one famous occasion, and loved good friendships and people at every level, especially children. He was no legalist: if someone needed healing on the Sabbath, he simply healed. He was not intolerant: he ate with hated publicans and obvious sinners. Nor was Jesus the namby-pamby, soft-and-sweet sort of person conjured up in so much art: he had an athletic vigor that could enable him to stay up all night in prayer or singlehandedly drive the money changers out of the Temple with a whip. He was a man totally committed to his mission of announcing the kingdom of God and then dying to make it all possible.

Even though future ages would enthrone him as the greatest individual who ever lived and Christians acclaim him as the God-

Israel Gov't. Tourist Office

Each Christmas, these bells in the tower of the Church of the Nativity at Bethlehem peal forth at midnight to announce the festival.

man, Jesus always had a sensitivity for the past, and he was continually quoting the Old Testament. One very luminous part of that past he could never forget, since Mary must have told him the story again and again, as mothers will. And even Jesus must have marveled at it, because he was so human: the story of angels over Bethlehem . . . the story of adoring shepherds and humbled wise men . . . the story of the first Christmas.

NOTES

1. A CAESAR'S CENSUS

ROMAN CENSUS IN EGYPT: This edict, from 104 A.D., begins: "Gaius Vibius Maximus, prefect of Egypt, says: The house-to-house census having started, it is essential that all persons who for any reason whatsoever are absent from their homes be summoned to return to their own hearths, in order that they may perform the customary business of registration. . . ." See A. H. M. Jones, ed., *A History of Rome Through the Fifth Century* (New York: Harper & Row, 1970), II, pp. 256 f.

AUGUSTUS: The harangue against the bachelors is recorded by Dio Cassius, *Roman History* (hereafter merely "Dio Cassius"), lvi, 1–10. The "Acts of Augustus" recording his censuses are *Res Gestae Divi Augusti,* 8. For the emperor's career, see Suetonius, *Divus Augustus;* Dio Cassius, li—lvi; Velleius Paterculus, *Compendium,* ii, 84–124.

JOSEPH BEN-IACOB, etc.: These reconstructions of their names mean "Joseph, son of Jacob" and "Mary, daughter of Joachim." For the identity of these fathers, see notes to chapters 10 and 11 below.

2. PALESTINE THE PARADOX

MOHAMMED'S TRIP TO JERUSALEM: *Sura,* xvii, 1 ff. in the Koran.

DEAD SEA AREA: The Hebrews called it the Salt Sea; the Greeks, the Asphalt Lake. See Strabo, *Geographica,* xvi, 2, 42. The destruction of Sodom and Gomorrah is related in Genesis 19.

3. A GALILEAN COUPLE

DEATH PENALTY FOR ADULTERY WITH BETROTHED: According to Deuteronomy 22:23: "If there is a betrothed virgin, and a man meets her in the city and lies with her, then you shall bring them both out to the gate of that city, and you shall stone them to death with stones. . . ."

MARRIAGE CUSTOMS: References to engagement and marriage in Biblical times are scattered widely across the Old and New Testaments. Extracanonical sources are: I Maccabees 9:39; Tobit, *passim.*

4. AN UNDATABLE DATE

DEATH OF HEROD: The chronology is discussed by Jack Finegan, *Handbook of Biblical Chronology* (Princeton, 1964), pp. 230 ff. See also W. E. Filmer, "The Chronology of the Reign of Herod the Great," *The Journal of Theological Studies,* XVII (October, 1966), 283–98.

CHRONOLOGY OF JESUS' LIFE: See Finegan, *op. cit.,* pp. 215 ff.; and Paul L. Maier, "Sejanus, Pilate, and the Date of the Crucifixion," *Church History,* XXXVII (March, 1968), 1–11.

QUIRINIUS: Tacitus, *Annals,* ii, 30; iii, 22, 23, 48; Suetonius, *Tiberius,* xlix; Dio Cassius, liv, 48; Josephus, *Antiquities,* xvii, 13, 5; xviii, 1, 1. For Quirinius and the census, see also: *Corpus inscriptionum Latinarum,* III, Suppl. 6687; Lily R. Taylor, "Quirinius and the Census of Judaea," *The American Journal of Philology,* 54 (1933), 120–33; Finegan, *op. cit.,* pp. 234–38; and A. N. Sherwin-White, *Roman Society and Roman Law in the New Testament* (Oxford: Clarendon, 1963), pp. 162–71. The last calls a provincial census of Judea during the reign of Herod the Great "an impossiblity" (p. 163), but Herod, as client-king, might easily have cooperated with Augustus' well-known proclivities for censuses in the provinces. See Tacitus, *Annals,* vi, 41.

SHEEP IN THE FIELDS MOST OF THE YEAR: The *Mishnah* has differing views on the length of time sheep spent in the wilderness, but *Bezah,* 40 a, suggests that they remained in the open both in the hot days and in the rainy season, i.e., all year round. See also *Shekalim,* vii, 4, and Alfred Edersheim, *The Life and Times of Jesus the Messiah* (Eerdmans, 1936), I, p. 186 f.—The statement of Stephen A. Haboush is from his letter to the author, January 23, 1971.

5. A BETHLEHEM GROTTO

DAVID AND BETHLEHEM: I Samuel 17:12 ff.; 20:6, 28; 16:1–13. The messianic ruler was also expected to hail from Bethlehem, according to Micah 5:2.

JESUS BORN IN A CAVE: Justin Martyr, *Dialogus,* lxxviii. Justin's reference to a cave as the site is also supported in the *Protevangelium of James,* xviii, 1 ff.

6. LOCAL SHEPHERDS, DISTANT MAGI

FLOCKS DESTINED FOR THE TEMPLE? Several Old Testament references suggest that the Messiah was expected to be revealed from *Migdal Eder,* "the tower of the flock" near the place where Jacob buried his wife Rachel (Gen. 35:19–21; Mic. 4:8). Tradition identifies *Migdal-eder* with the shepherds' village of Beit Sahur, near Bethlehem, and the *Mishnah* suggests that flocks pastured there were destined for Temple sacrifice. See *Shekalim,* vii, 4, and Edersheim, *loc. cit.*

BAR-COCHBA: led the Jewish revolt against Rome during the reign of the emperor Hadrian, but was killed by the Romans in 135 A.D. See Dio Cassius, lxix, 12–14; Eusebius, *Ecclesiastical History,* iv, 6.

SUETONIUS ON RULERS FROM JUDEA: *Divus Vespasianus,* iv.

7. AN INCREDIBLE STAR

THE STAR OF BETHLEHEM: For a summary of current scientific explanations, see Finegan, *op. cit.,* pp. 238–48; W. Burke-Gaffney, "Kepler and the Star of Bethlehem," *Journal of the Royal Astronomical Society of Canada,* XXXI (December, 1937), 417–25; and Roy K. Marshall, *The Star of Bethlehem* (U. of N. Carolina: Morehead Planetarium, 1963). The finest and most recent monograph arguing for planetary conjunction as explanation for the star is Konradin Ferrari d'Occhieppo, *Der Stern der Weisen* (Wien: Verlag Herold, 1969). This astronomer also suggests that zodiacal light might have appeared between Jupiter-Saturn and Bethlehem.

SATURN AS STAR OF ISRAEL: Amos 5:26, in which "Sakkuth" and "Kaiwan" are both names for the Babylonian Saturn. See also Tacitus, *Histories,* 5, 4.

THE WILLIAMS CATALOG: John Williams, *Observations of Comets from B.C. 611 to A.D. 1640 Extracted from the Chinese Annals* (London: Strangways and Walden, 1871).

8. HEROD THE KING

HEROD: Josephus, *Antiquities,* xiv, 9, 1—xvii, 8, 3; *Wars,* i, 10, 4—i, 33, 9. Matthew 2.

" . . . HEROD'S PIG . . .": Macrobius, *Saturnalia,* ii, 4.

9. UP TO JERUSALEM, DOWN TO EGYPT

THE ROBBER STORY: *Arabic Gospel of the Infancy,* xxiii. This and other apocryphal writings about Joseph, Mary, and the child Jesus are most conveniently available in text or outline form in Montague R. James, *The Apocryphal New Testament* (Oxford: Clarendon, 1924).

ARCHELAUS KILLS 3,000: Josephus, *Antiquities,* xvii, 9, 1–3.

10. JOSEPH THE CARPENTER

THE FATHER OF JOSEPH: is given as Jacob, son of Matthan, in Matthew's genealogy (1:15 f.), but as Heli, son of Matthat, in Luke's account (3:23 f.). The two genealogies are different up to David, after which they are identical back to Abraham. Various attempts to account for this divergence suggest that one is the legal, the other the natural descent of Joseph, or that Matthew gives the descent through Joseph's line, while Luke records it through Mary's.

DESTRUCTION OF SEPPHORIS: Josephus, *Antiquities,* xvii, 10, 5 and 9.

JESUS EXTENDS JOSEPH'S BEAMS: *Gospel of Thomas* (Greek A), xiii.

JOSEPH DIES AT 111: *History of Joseph the Carpenter,* x, xviii ff.

SISTERS OF JESUS: are named as Anna (or "Lysia") and Lydia in *History of Joseph the Carpenter,* ii.

11. MARY THE VIRGIN

THE FATHER OF MARY: is given as Joachim in Christian tradition (*Protevangelium of James,* i, 1 ff.). The name Heli (see above note on the father of Joseph) is the diminutive of Eliachim, which is an alternate form of Joachim. Therefore some scholars consider Luke's genealogy that of Mary herself and the name of her father in the *Protevangelium* substantiated. However, no definite name for Mary's father or mother is given in the New Testament.

" . . . AS IF SHE WERE A DOVE . . .": *Protevangelium,* viii, 1.

ANNUNCIATION AT THE WELL IN NAZARETH: "And she [Mary] took a pitcher and went forth to fill it with water. And behold, a voice said, 'Hail, thou that art highly favored, the Lord is with thee . . .' " (*Protevangelium,* xi, 1). But this apocryphon has the angel complete the Annunciation back in her home as she wove the Temple veil.

APOCRYPHAL VERSIONS OF MARY'S DEATH: Coptic and Syriac texts, as well as Greek and Latin narratives grouped under the title, The Passing of Mary, especially the *Transitus Sanctae Mariae.*

12. JESUS OF NAZARETH

TEMPLE VISIT AT AGE TWELVE: Luke 2:41–52.

JESUS AND THE FISH: *Gospel of Thomas* (Latin), i.

JESUS AND THE BIRDS: *Gospel of Thomas* (Greek A), ii.

JESUS SUPPOSEDLY CURSES A CHILD: *Gospel of Thomas* (Greek A), iv-v. The other childhood stories derive from this and other apocryphal infancy narratives.

JESUS' LINGUISTIC ABILITIES: Luke 4:17 ff.; John 8:6–8. Mark 7:26 ff. tells of the meeting with the Syrophoenician woman. The Latin terms in his recorded speech include: *modius* (Mt. 5:15); *quadrans* (Mt. 5:26); *legio* (Mt. 26:53).

PLOWS MADE BY JESUS: Justin Martyr, *Dialogus,* lxxxviii.

BRONZE STATUE OF JESUS: Eusebius, *Ecclesiastical History,* vii, 18.

75 10 9 8 7